Time to Live

The **Fiona Harrold** Coaching Series

Time

to Live
Francine Kaye

7 Steps to taming time

HODDER
MOBIUS

Copyright © 2005 by Francine Kaye

First published in Great Britain in 2005 by Hodder and Stoughton
A division of Hodder Headline

The right of Francine Kaye to be identified as the Author
of the Work has been asserted by her in accordance with the
Copyright, Designs and Patents Act 1988.

A Mobius Book

10 9 8 7 6 5 4 3 2 1

A CIP catalogue record for this title is
available from the British Library

ISBN 0 340 83705 5

Typeset in Stone Serif by Palimpsest Book Production Limited,
Polmont, Stirlingshire
Printed and bound by Clays Ltd, St Ives plc

Hodder Headline's policy is to use papers that are natural,
renewable and recyclable products and made from wood grown in
sustainable forests. The logging and manufacturing processes are expected
to conform to the environmental regulations of the country of origin.

Hodder and Stoughton Ltd
A division of Hodder Headline
338 Euston Road
London NW1 3BH

Quotation from *Scottish Himalayan Expedition* with acknowledgement
from JM Dent, a division of The Orion Publishing Group. All reasonable
efforts have been made to contact copyright holders.

Contents

Acknowledgements

My thanks and deep respect go to Fiona Harrold, who never doubts my abilities and holds me to the highest standards. I'm looking forward to many more years of fun and learning together.

Thank you, Gary. I would not be where I am today without you. Your encouragement and total support is awesome. Together forever my darling.

Thank you also to my fabulous children: Carly, for your love and friendship and Alex, for reminding me how important it is to make time for hugs no matter how busy we are. You help me make our lives work together and I am so proud of you both.

Special thanks to Simon Maurer, for seeing in me so much more than was on the surface and inviting me to play a bigger game. May your light always shine.

Thanks to Sheila Crowley at AP Watt and to all at Hodder and Stoughton, particularly my editor, Helen Coyle, for taking the time to understand where I was 'coming from'.

And finally, thank you to my courageous clients who made a choice to make time to live.

Foreword from Fiona Harrold

This is the best book I've ever read on time management. Seriously. If you've ever felt you needed to get more of a handle on your life, read this book. This is no dull, time-efficiency manual. Francine has identified all the everyday ways that we lose time and end up feeling frustrated and she'll help you to pinpoint where you're going wrong and how you may be making life harder for yourself. Do you ever find it hard to say 'No' to other people's requests, do things you aren't enthusiastic about, take on too much, delegate badly, procrastinate; or are you a bit of a perfectionist? Do you know what's really, really important to you in life? Are you on course to accomplish your true passion and purpose? This is what you'll get to grip with on these pages.

Francine gives us practical solutions to all of these issues and challenges and much, much more. She's written an 'unput-downable' guide to help you get more of what you want out of life, and far less of what you don't want. I give you my personal guarantee that everything you read here works – brilliantly – because I receive emails from Francine's private clients every week thanking me for recommending her and sharing the terrific improvements they've made to their lives with her by their side. Francine has been an invaluable member of my coaching team for five years and she is one of the smartest, most dedicated coaches on the planet. Use her as your personal guide to upgrade your own situation. Come and meet her on our website and share your success with us, at www. fionaharrold.com. Enjoy making time to live. You'll thank yourself you did.

Good Luck!

Fiona Harrold
London 2005

1

Where Is My Time Going?

This time, like all times, is a very good one if we but know what to do with it

RALPH WALDO EMERSON

How often do you have the kind of day when everything gets done? I'll bet it's the kind of day you'd like to have more often. A day like this happens when you are most in control of your time, when you know what you want, are motivated to achieve it and breeze through the day on focus and on time. You have of course accepted that you cannot control all the events in your life, but you know you have the personal power to choose how you react to them and in doing so you are easily able to manage your time and your life.

The key to successful life management is making the right choices about how you spend the minutes and hours in your day. From morning till night, we unconsciously make moment-to-moment choices that shape our destinies. Every mouthful of food you consume dictates how you will feel and look in the coming days. Every task you undertake either takes you nearer to your goals or further away from them. Every decision you make, however minuscule, can either take your life in the direction you want it to go or move you away from the life you desire. People who are successful with time have made the emotional connection that allows them to choose where they invest their time and the results they want to achieve. Not only do these people understand that time is their most precious commodity and trade their time wisely, they also understand how to choose the emotions that will guarantee their effective management of time, which will in turn guarantee success in whatever they choose to do.

We all know people who are simply life's winners. The kind of people who just get out there and do it. There are others who seem to observe from the sidelines, never playing full out on the pitch of life, always watching others achieve their goals. And then there are those who never seem to have time for anything; time takes flight and they miss the plane.

So, why is it that some of us are more effective with our time than others? What is the special ingredient that successful people have that can make any one of us terrific at taming time?

ULTIMATE TIME TAMERS

In spring 1963, in Dallas, Texas, after retiring from a successful twenty-five-year career in direct sales, Mary Kay decided to write a book using her experience to advise women how to survive in a man's world. In the process, she found she was actually creating her dream company. She envisioned a company where women would be allowed to pursue unlimited opportunities, each controlling their own independent business. In a few short months she invested her life savings, recruited several sales people, had her products sourced and was ready to open shop. In September 1963 Mary Kay Cosmetics was founded. Eight months later she had to expand her warehouse and within five years Mary Kay Cosmetics Inc. was listed on the public stock exchange. Mary Kay's philosophy was 'Nothing wilts faster than a laurel rested upon.' She said that 'one intense hour is worth a whole dreamy day,' and got up at 5 a.m. each morning to make the most of every minute of her day. Mary Kay knew that time was precious and never wasted a moment putting her vision into action. By 1994 she was listed for the second time in the *Fortune 500*, had added another thirty years of incredible productivity to a career she had retired from in 1963, and said of herself that she was 'just an ordinary women with extraordinary determination'. Mary Kay Ash died in November 2001, leaving behind a legacy of people who continue to share her dream to enrich women's lives around the world.

In October 1996 Lance Armstrong, the Olympic cyclist, was diagnosed with testicular cancer at the age of twenty-four. He was already on his way to becoming a sporting legend but the doctors gave him only a 40 per cent chance of survival. They said he might never walk again and would never have children. A young man, whose career depended on split-second timing to win the race, faced watching time run out on him in a race he could not win. One year later, after surviving a rollercoaster of brain surgery and chemotherapy when he constantly faced life and death, he decided to try to race again. His training was disciplined, timed and balanced, with healthy food and plenty of rest. Just sixteen months after being discharged from hospital he entered the Tour de France and won in the fastest time ever. A few months later he became a father. The man who did everything at a fast cadence is now much more thoughtful and reflective. He has his life back. He has more time to live. Like the title of his biography, he has learned something very precious about the time in his life: he knows *It's Not About the Bike*.

At four years old Maria Sharapova picked up a racket and started to play tennis. By five she was already playing in an exhibition tournament in Moscow and was spotted by the tennis legend Martina Navratilova, who recommended that her parents take her to Nick Bollettieri's tennis academy in the United States. Maria and her father travelled to Miami and, uninvited, they went straight to Bollettieri's academy in Bradenton, Florida. One of Bollettieri's coaches agreed to take Maria on to the court and with her first stroke he was blown away by her ability. At the age of nine, Maria began a two-year separation from her mother – the result of visa restrictions and the family's financial situation – and began intensive training at the Bollettieri academy. Maria said of that time, 'When I came to the United States it wasn't easy for me. I didn't see my mum for two years and I barely saw my dad for one year. I was living in a dormitory by myself and sacrificed a lot of things.'

Maria turned professional on her fourteenth birthday in 2001. By 2003 she had rapidly risen up the rankings. She made her grand slam debut in the Australian Open and she qualified for the French Open. Then, after reaching the semi-finals at Edgbaston, she progressed to the fourth round at Wimbledon, the best-ever performance by a female wild card. Maria won her first titles on the World Tennis Association tour in Japan and Quebec and ended the year ranked 32.

By 2004 Maria had won £300,000 from her playing career and went on to stun the tennis world by defeating Serena Williams in the singles finals at Wimbledon to win the prestigious tournament at the age of seventeen. Maria says, 'My drive and determination comes from my Russian blood.'

How is that Mary Kay, Lance Armstrong and Maria Sharapova were able to make the most impactful use of their time? What was the vital ingredient that allowed them to do this?

TIME-TAMING PRINCIPLES

It's very simple! They, like every other person who is successful with time, understood the key element that is fundamental to taming time. *They knew their outcome.* They all had the ability to focus on what was most important. Added to this, they all had an unstoppable attitude. They held a clear vision of the quality of life they wanted for themselves and those around them, and would not be distracted from achieving their individual outcomes. This intoxicating combination gave them the motivation to move mountains. There was no procrastination. They had a powerful purpose that they had been preparing for over many years. They were ready for action.

This simple strategy is all you need to achieve absolutely anything you want in your own life. It's a strategy that every one of us has the ability to follow and one that ultimately gives you power with time.

You don't have to be a world-standard tennis player, a cosmetics queen or wait until some life-threatening disease becomes your alarm call in order to reach your goals, achieve success, and live the life you want. Any limitations that you perceive right now, those obstacles that get in your way: be prepared to set fire to them. I am going to show you how to redesign your time. You are going to learn what's most important to you to enable you to choose your outcome, focus your attention and take actions that give you what you want every time so that you can get the most satisfaction out of your life each and every day.

Knowing your outcome is the vital ingredient you must master for intelligent time management. When you know your outcome you will be growing towards a compelling future that motivates and inspires you on a daily basis. Knowing your outcome allows you to focus on what's most important at any given moment, which will permit you to transform your dreams and desires into achievable day-by-day steps. Knowing your outcome is the first rung of your success ladder. Don't even bother to step up until you know your outcome because you may climb to the top only to find that your ladder was leaning against the wrong wall. If you don't know your own outcome, you'll always be working towards someone else's. Creating a compelling outcome will keep you focused as you take positive actions towards your undoubtable success. Knowing your outcome is also one of the first rules of effective goal-setting, which we will look at in more detail later on.

What else do you need?

The next ingredient is *attitude*. Your attitude is far more important than aptitude. You can always learn a new skill, but an 'I can' and "I will" attitude is what you need to be successful with time, and I expect nothing less from you. In 1982 I read a book that had the most powerful impact on my thinking. It changed the way I viewed what was achievable in a lifetime and what human beings are really capable of. That book was *Man's Search For Meaning* by Viktor Frankl, a Holocaust survivor. For me, his words were light bulbs that illuminated what it takes to overcome anything and survive. I knew that I would never be able to make excuses for my life ever again. Viktor Frankl said that anything can be taken away from a person except their attitude – how they choose to respond to any given situation. How could someone subjected to the daily degradation of a concentration camp have the strength and conviction to think in this way? Viktor Frankl had realised that he had the ability to choose how he responded to the insanity surrounding him. I find it astonishing that he could hold on to the thought of a better future and change his attitude towards his fellow man and his own situation in such circumstances.

All of us at one time or another forget that we have the power to choose our attitudes. We spend our time justifying why we cannot achieve our goals. We would rather be right about why we believe we can't do something than do what it takes to move our lives to the next level. Whenever I find myself thinking negatively about anything, I remember Viktor Frankl and I know in my soul that if he could change his attitude in a moment, then so can I and so can you.

Finally there is *action*. Nothing was ever achieved without taking the appropriate action. Sounds obvious, doesn't it, yet one of the biggest threats to effective time management is personal procrastination. It's not that we don't know how to take action; but sometimes, we get stuck in our comfortable ruts, running our lives on automatic pilot, resigned to mediocre results. Without action nothing changes, thoughts stay as thoughts, dreams remain fantasies that other people achieve. Action is everything: new actions, different actions, more effective actions. Appropriately timed and decisive action is what it takes to achieve the results you want.

HOW TO USE THIS BOOK

This book is based on the three main principles outlined above. Effectively managing your time is about knowing what to focus on at any given moment. Whatever you focus on always moves you towards an outcome of some kind, so you need to know what you want that outcome to be before you arrive. Your attitude is simply how you react to all the things that happen in your life and what you make them mean. Your belief about the meaning ultimately dictates what actions you will take as a result. The following chapters will help you to understand that time is not just about the hours in your day. You are going to discover that using your time productively and effectively is based on an underlying ingredient that, when added, gives you the perfect recipe for successful time management in every area of your life.

Ideally, each chapter serves as a week's work. At the end of each chapter there are questions, some of which may take several days to answer. To get the most value from the book, I suggest you read it through first and then go back to answer the questions within each chapter and then do The Work at the end of each chapter. You'll notice that I have referred to both work and general life situations. The guidelines offered apply to every life situation, not just to those of us who are paid for the work we do. By the end of this book you will have created a focused living plan which specifically relates to how you can get the best out of your time in every circumstance.

TIME OUT

We all at some time in our lives need to reassess. Life is not a dress rehearsal. This is it. If you waste a day you can't get it back. Unlike the lottery, there is no rollover. I learned this the hard way years ago.

When I was newly divorced with two young children,

my entire focus was to create a stable environment in which to bring up my kids. Another priority was to create a sustainable income. I had not worked full-time for nearly ten years and the thought of having to go back to an office appalled me. However, I went. With no family nearby, I relied on two lovely paid 'aunties', without whose help I'd have been lost. By the time I came home from work, though, it was suppertime and bath time and bedtime and my life was on automatic pilot. During the evenings I continued studying and although I was already a coach, I did not think I could create enough income to leave my office-bound job. Days were eighteen hours long, I had no balance between work and home, no personal fulfilment and, worst of all, I realised that my original purpose (my outcome), to be a great mum and create this wonderful home for my children, was falling apart right in front of me. I was drained and exhausted trying to keep all the balls in the air and I knew that if I did not get off the treadmill voluntarily, then my body would eventually make me.

So after grappling with my gremlins, I set fire to my fears, marched in to my CEO's office and handed in my notice. I cannot explain the relief I felt. I knew that achieving balance in my life was of utmost importance. I'd missed enough years of not being there for my children and I wasn't about to miss any more. I also needed to do the work I was born to do and have some time for me. However, I'll not pretend it was easy at first. With financial pressures and only myself to rely on, I needed to be disciplined with my day. One of the first things I did was to find out about a time-management course. I was not prepared to tolerate eighteen-hour days any more. I wanted to get everything done and still have time for the kids. The course sounded so great, offering tools that were invaluable, but I could not afford it. How could I turn this around? What kind of unstoppable attitude would I need to pull out of the bag? Amazingly, I managed to convince the course manager that I would make a superb trainer and persuaded him to give me the course for free as well as training me to teach others these vital skills. To my surprise he agreed and within three months I was out in the field teaching other people to manage their time and earning money in the process.

TIME POWER

If I can regain control of my time and create a life that works for me, then I know you can too. I'd never expect you to do anything I hadn't done myself. So, I am going to give you a foolproof time-management toolkit. I guarantee that if you use these tools consistently your life will change dramatically. Now is the time for you to redesign your time, explode your personal productivity and effectiveness and get back into balance.

At first it will be like using any new muscle. You'll need to put in some conscious effort to build strength. You wouldn't expect to go to the gym, do one great workout and be fit for the rest of your life. The price you pay for guaranteed success is paid in advance and in full, so it's important you know the price and are willing to pay it. I promise it will be worth it.

IT'S JUST A PERFECT DAY . . .

How would you feel if at the end of the day you looked back and realised it had been something like this?

Today was really great. I got up at 6.45 a.m. after having just the right amount of sleep. I took a twenty-minute power walk and then jumped in the shower, leaving enough time to have juice, coffee and a fresh warmed croissant. Leaving five minutes earlier for work meant that I did not get stressed in the traffic. On the way I listened to my new motivational tape and arrived at the office inspired and fired up for the day ahead.

A new pile of work was already waiting for me. As I had cleared my desk the night before, I moved it to one side, taking my usual fifteen minutes to plan my day before beginning to prioritise the pile. Because I have several deadlines this week and meetings to attend, I am aware that there is only so much time available for the projects I need to complete. I made sure that I considered this during my planning time.

As usual the day presented me with unexpected situations, which had to be dealt with in a way that accounted for everyone's needs. They were no problem – I used my Powerful Focused Questions and got them handled.

At lunch I met a friend for a snack and some fresh air and then went back to the office to complete the afternoon on time. I don't work late now. Seems ages since I did – there's just no need now that I am the master of my time.

I went straight to the gym on the way home from work, met the guys for a drink after my workout and then went home to the meal that I had left out of the freezer this morning. I didn't watch TV as I wanted to read my new book and after two chapters are complete I am ready for bed.

Does this sound like the type of day you had? No? But it can be! Don't get me wrong, I'm not expecting you to be a superhero when you have to take into account the kids, maybe elderly parents, a demanding boss and client deadlines, but I do believe that time can actually be on your side if you know how to tame it.

First and foremost, though, you need to understand what time really is.

WHAT IS TIME?

There is no more physical time for anyone. Rich or poor, happy or sad, we all have exactly the same amount of time 24/7. The only way of managing your time is by deciding what's most important in any moment. You'll hear me repeat this many times. That's because it's the key to understanding successful time management.

You get to be awake on average for around seventeen to eighteen hours a day. This means, unless you can survive on very little sleep, you have the same amount of time to 'spend' each day.

Let me make this even clearer. Life expectancy, although on the increase, still stands at seventy. Living the full span gives you 840 months' worth of time to 'spend' from birth. A third is spent asleep. By thirty-five years old, half your quota is spent. You now have 280 waking months left to live. Are you beginning to get the picture?

Life is extremely short. Time is our most precious commodity, And yet, how many people out there are sleepwalking their way through their lives, or watching the clock and wishing it was Friday? Thankfully, you are not among them, but if you have ever felt this way, make a decision, right here and now, not to waste another moment. Start allowing yourself to imagine doing satisfying and fulfilling work that is productive and effective. Ask yourself what a balanced and happy life would look like. How would it feel to spend your time in that way?

EMOTIONAL TIME: THE ULTIMATE INGREDIENT

In order for you to answer the above questions and get some idea of what your ideal life would be like, you have to take time to explore your feelings. Feelings play a big part in how we manage our time. Remember I talked about the underlying ingredient that allows anyone to be successful with their time? Well, this is it. Although we use the clock and calendar to measure time, I don't believe that this really describes the *essence* of time. I believe that *time is an emotion*. Ever wondered why time goes so quickly when you are absorbed and yet seems to drag by so slowly when you are bored? It's all about how you feel, *your emotional response* to what you are doing in the moment.

For example, when you do too much of what you don't value, you feel stressed (an *emotion*). If you don't do what you think you should do, you may feel guilty (an *emotion*). It's our emotional response to how we spend our time that makes time such an evocative subject.

When people come to time management, one of the main outcomes they want to achieve is less stress. Stress is an emotional response to spending your time in situations that are extremely uncomfortable for you; its ingredients can include being physically and mentally exhausted, upset, angry, disappointed or frustrated. This can happen at work and in your private life and if it happens regularly, eventually you'll have to address the situation or your body will almost certainly make you do so by breaking down.

It is my belief that the key to effective time management lies in understanding and choosing your emotions. Mary Kay, Lance Armstrong and Maria Sharapova all understood that in order to make the most of every hour in each day they had to master their emotions, adopt the appropriate attitude and focus on their outcomes in order to become masters of their time.

REACTION MANAGEMENT

Once we feel something, our next automatic step is a reaction to that feeling. It's our minute-by-minute emotional reactions to events that make the most impact on our day. Remember the last time you were late for an important meeting, or for work. What state of mind were you in when you arrived?

I recently arrived on time for a meeting to discuss a time-management programme, only to discover that the main decision-maker was held up and would be late. When he arrived he was flustered and distracted, and I wondered what I could do to make him be fully present and attentive. I made eye contact with him and asked him what it was like being late. He was quite shocked by this question, and immediately went into a justification, explaining that his last meeting had overrun, and then the train was late and kept stopping in tunnels. As a result, he had had to run from the station and arrived for our meeting hot, agitated and uncomfortable. I asked him if there was anything else he felt about being late. He smiled and rose to my further challenge and told me that he felt he had shown disrespect to his two colleagues and me and this really wasn't his style. His whole day would now be out of sync and anyway he had known it was going to be a bad day when he overslept by fifteen minutes. Phew! I was exhausted listening to him!

I thanked him for his honesty and here's what I told him.

You must learn to separate what actually happens from what you make it mean.

Look back at his story. What *actually happened* was that he was late for the meeting. He could give me several justifications for this, some of his own choosing, some out of his control. But he could not change the outcome: late to the meeting. I explained that if you cannot change the 'what actually happened', then you must change your reaction: the 'what you make it mean'.

He had made it 'mean' that he was disrespectful and

now the rest of the day would be 'out of sync'. I pointed out that this meaning would now impact the physical and emotional quality of the rest of his day based *entirely* on his emotional reactions to what had happened. This was quite a revelation to him and his colleagues, and once they understood the formula, they came up with their own examples of things that 'had happened' and what they 'made it mean'. I was able to reiterate the emotional and physical costs of their reactions. I showed them how the quality of the conversations they were having in their heads defined the quality of their everyday lives.

Understanding your own emotional reactions to 'what happens' each day will be your greatest tool in deciding how to manage your time. If you get nothing else from this book, except fully understanding this ultimate ingredient, you will become more effective with your time than you could ever have dreamed possible

---

While understanding that the way we experience time is based on emotion, it is, of course, important to have some practical tools that allow us to put our emotions to their best use to get the results we want. There are some vital distinctions that underpin deciding what we do with our time.

ATTENTION MANAGEMENT

We know that there is no more 'physical' time available for any of us, and people who are successful with time will tell you that you *must focus on what's most important at any given moment.*

Since what you focus on is simply what you pay attention to, you must become aware of some important distinctions.

You must know the difference between *urgent* and *important.*

For example:

- The doorbell rings during your weekly family dinner: is it urgent or important?
- Your boss wants an item *now*: is that urgent or important?
- If the telephone rings in the middle of your favourite TV programme is that urgent or important?

Are you having trouble with any of these? Have you started off any of your thoughts with, 'Well if?' Then, guess what, you don't know the difference between urgent and important yet.

The only answer to all these situations is, 'Yes'! They are all urgent.

Here's why. Anything that happens *right now*, in the moment, is urgent. The definition of urgent, according to the *Concise Oxford Dictionary*, is 'calling for immediate action or attention'. The most important word here is 'calling'. All these scenarios may be 'calling' very loudly but the real skill comes in defining whether they are *important* or not and then responding effectively. For example, if your boss wants an item now, it's pretty clear that it's urgent and important, this is your boss we are talking about. However, when the doorbell rings during dinner, or the telephone rings in the middle of your favourite TV programme, it's urgent because it happens now, but it's possible that these are not important interruptions. When you understand the difference between urgent and important you are more able to choose your reaction rather than respond automatically.

THE WORK

1. Make distinctions. Before every task you undertake this week, ask yourself, is it:

- Urgent and important?
- Urgent?
- Important?
- Not urgent and not important?

The more often you ask yourself the question, the clearer you'll be about your responses in your own mind. And once you're clear in your mind, you can decide what action to take.

2. Keep a time log. Keep a time log for at least three consecutive days so you know exactly where and how you spend your time. Draw up a table using these headings or create your own. Be meticulous in recording everything: you may be surprised by what you discover!

For example:

Time	Task/activity	Time completed	Comments
9.30	Planning day	9.45	I now know 'what's most important' today.
9.45	Coffee and chat with boss	9.58	Surprised this took so long
10.00	Writing report	11.00	Completed report before deadline – feeling relieved!

By taking these action steps and making your comments, you will raise your daily awareness of your own emotional reactions to what happens, you'll be more aware of how much time tasks take and you'll have more clarity to decide where you want to put your focus.

Key Idea

This week ask yourself regularly: If I focus my attention only on producing the most important results, what would I have to say no to?

2

Values and Beliefs

I've had a wonderful time, but this wasn't it

GROUCHO MARX

Isn't that sometimes the truth? Have you ever felt as if you were living the wrong life, as if you had been handed a script for a part you never auditioned for? How often have you spent days or evenings or even whole weekends doing things and being with people that did not inspire you? It's almost certainly because you did not value what you were doing or had different values to the people with whom you were spending your time.

> Understanding your values is the key to making the right decisions about how and where you spend your time. Wasting your time not living in alignment with your personal values causes all your frustrations and upsets.

This chapter works on the following assumption: unless you spend your time doing what inspires and motivates you and live each day in alignment with your own personal values it is most unlikely that you will ever be truly satisfied or fulfilled. If you are not satisfied or fulfilled then you are wasting both your time and your life. So before you can create any goals, make any choices or decisions and take any action, it's vital that you first build a solid foundation of your personal values.

Imagine life is like building a house. The first thing you must have in place are solid foundations so that you can put up the walls, create a raintight roof and move in. Now, just suppose your house is built on sand. Pretty soon it will fall down around your ears. It's the same with your life. Until you understand that your values form the solid foundations on which to build your life, you will always be trying to build a house on sand.

A value is a 'must have' in your life. It's a fact that when what you do and what you value marry together, you experience your highest level of productivity both at work and in your life. Only then will you reach the balance vital to achieving success and fulfilment in all you do. Your values will act as your compass, which guide you towards the successful achievement of your goals. Your values will underpin your goals.

Most of us are not islands. We live with other people, we work with other people, and we have friends and family. We negotiate our lives with all the other people we come into contact with on a daily basis. Knowing your values will help you to identify how to respond to people. Using your values as a reference, you'll become aware of those people who fit into your life and those who don't. Similarly, you can use your values as a guide to enable you to respond to problems and opportunities. You'll begin to notice which value is not being honoured rather than becoming defensive and you'll know very quickly whether you want to take up a new opportunity or whether it is a waste of your precious time.

Taking time to understand your values helps you to create a strong sense of direction. This 'inner compass' will always point you towards your route to happiness and fulfilment. Your values will allow you to discover your purpose in life; in fact I don't know a more fabulous way of eliciting your life purpose than by using your values as a guide.

By aligning your values with what you do and how you respond and behave, you'll experience a flow to your life that doesn't require you to 'wade through porridge', as one client recently put it.

WHAT ARE YOUR VALUES?

There are several different ways of uncovering your values. I find the method described below extremely effective as a means to pull your values apart and understand their components.

- Create a list of what you 'must have' in your life. For example must you have: respect/creativity/growth/ independence/a relationship/integrity? Make sure the words you use to describe your 'must haves' are your words. 'Honesty' is a word that is used so often, but you may describe 'honesty' as 'truthfulness' or 'transparency'. Use a word that fits comfortably with you. Come up with a list of around ten to fifteen 'must haves' in your own life.
- Put your 'must haves' into actions. For example, 'respect' becomes 'be respectful'; 'independence' becomes 'be independent'; 'be in a relationship'; 'grow spiritually'; 'have integrity'; 'work creatively'.
- Create a paragraph for each value. For example, 'Be independent'. Independently take full responsibility for myself without relying on others. Allow my children to exercise independence. Make my own choices at all times and respect other people's choices.

- Prioritise your values using the Time to Live method: A=vital, B=important, C=some value. This can sometimes prove tricky, but just ask yourself which value, if you could not honour it, would make you most crazy. You may discover that unless you have your independence, it's pretty hard for you to be in relationship. Play with this exercise until it feels and looks right to you.
- Pay attention to whether your performance at work and out of work aligns with your values. Notice where you compromise your values and where you honour them. Be aware of your experience of both.
- Decide to start living in line with your personal values and watch your life be transformed.

Values keep you going when the going gets tough. When you know what you value most in life in order of priority, then you'll have your own unique set of tools to help you to choose how you live, what work is right for you, and what you are willing to compromise on or not.

Once you understand your values and have decided to live by them fully, the only obstacle that can stand in your way of doing so is whether you believe it is possible. The way you manage your time and live your life depends upon your personal belief system combined with how you experience time on a day-to-day basis.

BEYOND BELIEF

Have you any idea how powerful your beliefs are? Just look around at our world. Everything that happens is based on what human beings believe. Every innovation has been created because someone believed it was possible; every success story is based on a personal belief that it could happen; all the wars, all the arguments about religion occur because people have powerful beliefs; and every time we make peace it is because people believe that living together is better than tearing each other apart. Personal beliefs have the power to create, as well as the power to destroy. Human beings are constantly translating what happens in their lives into what they make it mean. Your belief about these meanings can either empower you and everyone around you or it can pull you down and take the world with it.

The beliefs that you hold about yourself and others become your operating principles. You have been living on the basis that these beliefs are true, that they carry conviction, that they are reasonable and justified. Our constant challenge is to understand whether our beliefs serve ourselves or others, or if they are simply obstacles that stand in our way.

I'm not suggesting you should show any disrespect to the source of these beliefs. Mostly they were created, either by you or someone else, to serve you in some way. What I'm asking you to do is question whether they still serve you today. If they don't, let them go. Don't allow them to prevent you from spending your precious time living your life your way. For example, a belief in the value of becoming healthy and wealthy is an asset to you, not a detraction. It gives you the choice to inspire and help others. Your newfound wealth might allow you to contribute to society and your newfound health to have the energy to do more to make your world a better place. Decide right now that you are going to make clear distinctions between beliefs that serve and beliefs that don't. This is not about what you can or cannot do, or what you consider to be possible or impossible; it's more about what you believe about who you are. If you believe you can – you will. If you believe you can't – well, you just won't.

Your beliefs are the difference between you being effective in any area of your life or becoming a 'should've been'. This is the case in every area of our lives. The following belief-busters are your first step to getting more effective with the hours in your day.

BELIEF-BUSTERS

> Remember, happiness doesn't depend upon who you are
> or what you have, it depends solely upon what you think
> DALE CARNEGIE

What would have to happen in order for you to be satisfied with the way you manage your time right now? What beliefs do you hold on to that are the source of your answers?

For example, if you think that getting up earlier would allow you to manage your time more effectively but you never manage to get out of bed when the alarm goes off, what is it you believe about yourself that stops you? It could be that you believe you are lazy, that you need a certain amount of sleep, that you are not a 'morning' person. All these beliefs would stand in the way of you getting out of bed at 6 a.m. instead of 7 a.m. These kinds of beliefs, about anything from being more organised, about planning ahead, about dieting or exercising, are obstacles that block you from getting what you want out of your life.

So what would you have to believe in order to be more effective in your life?

Take a moment to think about what you don't have enough time for. Write down at least five areas that, if you made time for them, would make a real difference to the quality of your life. Examples are planning time, exercise, learning a new skill or pastime. Now ask yourself the following questions:

- What do I believe now that stops me doing any of the above?
- What would I have to believe in order to include the above in my life?
- What else would I have to believe in order for me to make it happen?
- If I believed that, what would I do?
- When will I do it?

Find your motivation for changing your limiting belief and visualise your outcome. Take action and do not allow yourself the luxury of falling back into that old comfort zone of past beliefs that keeps you playing small. There is truth in the adage 'no pain no gain'.

OTHER PEOPLE'S VALUES

Your values are an intrinsic part of your being, as are everyone else's. That's quite tricky because you'll quickly discover that other people don't always value the same things you do. This can lead to a values collision or conflict.

One client, Claire, a City analyst, places huge value

on punctuality. She works to deadlines and is never without her personal organiser. She always arrives five minutes early and phones exactly when she says she will. Claire has a close circle of four friends, one of whom, Joanne, is always late, makes no excuse and has left Claire waiting outside tube stations and restaurants in the cold on numerous occasions. So Claire told me that after realising that Joanne is violating one of her top values, she has decided to end their friendship, as 'Joanne shows me no respect by continuously turning up late'. Does this sound familiar to you in any way? Have you ever ended a friendship or business arrangement because the other person kept letting you down and dishonoured one of your top values?

I challenged Claire to speak to Joanne and tell her that when she continuously turns up late, Claire feels that Joanne does not respect her or value their friendship. During their conversation, this is what Claire discovered. Joanne does not have a 'punctuality' value. She is the same with everyone. She does not wear a watch because she does not want to be 'controlled' by time. She has a spontaneous free spirit, a flexible job as a musician and does not see time in the same way Claire does. Claire was surprised at her own response to her friend's revelations. She reported that it was like a light had been turned on for her. By understanding her own values, Claire could see Joanne's values shining through. However, one mutual value emerged in the conversation. Joanne does *respect* Claire and certainly does not want to lose her friendship. Claire has great fun with Joanne and would miss her laughter and spontaneity. Both friends decided to make new arrangements for meeting in the future that will serve them both. Joanne will meet Claire inside the restaurant or venue where she can have a drink and read her paper. Joanne will try to modify her behaviour out of respect for Claire and Claire will be more tolerant if Joanne is not more than fifteen minutes late.

When you have values conflicts *with other people* the key is good communication. Once people understand the impact their behaviour has on you and how it makes you feel, they are more willing to listen and create a win-win situation for you both. When a relationship is threatened in any way, nine times out of ten it's a values conflict. By listening for the other person's values, you will be able to create a platform from which to sort out your differences without compromising either one of you. This will save you so much wasted time and energy and leave you free to do what's really important.

PERSONAL VALUES CONFLICTS

> At work you think of the children you have left at home. At home you think of the work you've left unfinished. Such a struggle is unleashed within yourself. Your heart is rent
>
> GOLDA MEIR

Sometimes we experience a conflict between our own values. When it happens we feel torn. For example, if you value 'security' highly and are starting your own business, how will you manage the inevitable risk factor? If you value environment and work for a company with no such scruples, you'll be torn between your fundamental values and the carrot of that impending promotion.

In such circumstances you'll need to re-examine the true, current importance of your value. You certainly don't want to hold yourself back from achieving your goals, but neither do you want to experience inner struggle or anxiety.

Look for five examples of conflicting values in your own life and then ask yourself these clarifying questions to help you solve the conflict:

- Am I clinging on to my value out of habit, or fear?
- Is this my value or somebody else's?

- Does this value really serve an essential purpose for me right now?
- What would need to happen in order for me to . . . (For example, branch out into my own business, but be responsible for my security? Enter into a new relationship but keep my independence, or elevate my career and still be there for my family? Use your own examples to ask yourself this question.)

IN OR OUT OF TIME

As well as our beliefs about ourselves, there is another aspect of how we mentally operate that can have a powerful impact on how we experience time in our lives.

During the 1970s Richard Bandler and John Grinder created Neuro Linguistic Programming. NLP uses techniques and strategies that examine how human beings make sense of their experience of the world and how they interact with others. One NLP theory is that we all have an internal 'time line' which dictates how we experience time. What's interesting is that some people naturally have an 'in-time' perspective. This means that they live more for the thrill of the moment and find it harder to visualise the future or see how the past and the present relate to it. Other people have a 'through time' perspective. This means they are more able to see the bigger picture and are often good planners because they are more aware of future consequences. Each has its own value. Both work on a time line going from one point to another.

Along with your values and your beliefs, understanding whether you are an 'in-time' or 'through-time' person will allow you to make empowering choices about how you spend your time.

So how do you know which you are? NLP provides a simple exercise for working this out. Point your finger to where you imagine the future to be. Now point your finger to where you believe the past to be. Did you point directly in front of you for the future and directly behind you to the past? Then you are almost certainly an in-time person. Did you point to the right for the future and to the left for the past? Chances are you are a through-time person. While there is room for slight variation, people's time lines usually fall into either of these categories.

In-Time People

In-time people seem to live more in the present. I would class myself as naturally in-time. I'm spontaneous and live life to the full in the moment. I often find it hard to keep an eye on the time because I am so immersed in what I am doing. Coaching time management for me is a bit like 'physician heal thyself'; it keeps me much more aware of where I focus my time. Another challenge for me is planning ahead. As the future is right in front of me, looking ahead and being aware of the consequences of my actions today for my distant future is a challenge. I need to make an effort to consider how my decisions today will affect my life in five years' time. My other challenge lies with the past. Because it's behind me, it's almost inaccessible. This means that, once again, I must be conscious in the moment not to repeat old patterns that do not serve me.

Through-Time People

James, a financial planner, is a through-time person. James points to a past on the left and to a future on his right. This means that he has much more of a spatial awareness of time. He sees the bigger picture. He plans his time fabulously and is extremely well organised. He doesn't get overwhelmed with the here and now. Because he has taken the time to consider his actions based on a clearer vision of the past and future, life does not hold as many surprises. James brings clarity to his thinking and does not rush into solutions or decisions. He tends to take more time to clarify, digest and think things through. He is not naturally spontaneous, preferring to make choices in a more measured way.

A combination of both in-time and through-time thinking is of course ideal and needs to be cultivated in order to be more effective with time. However, it's important for you to know how you naturally operate so that you don't have a sense of acting out of sync with yourself. Once you recognise your natural way of being then you can choose to add qualities and values that will serve you in managing your time. What we do know, however, is that living in the past or worrying about a future that has not yet happened does not serve us either. You cannot change your past and you cannot predict the future. You cannot live in F.E.A.R. (Future Expectations Appearing Real). What you can do is live effectively in the present at any given moment, making choices and decisions that take you into tomorrow with ease and without worry.

THE WORK

1. Get familiar with your values. Understand what you must have in life for happiness and fulfilment. Is it success, family, relationship, challenge, adventure, security? List your values and then put them in order of priority.

2. Notice when you are not honouring your values. If you spend your time in places and in ways that are not in alignment with your values, is it any wonder that you never seem to have enough time for the things you really want to do?

3. Understand how your personal beliefs impact the quality of time in your life. Do you believe you have time to work out and prepare healthy meals? Do you believe that you can say no to people and tasks that compromise your values? Take some time to list your beliefs and question whether they serve you or sabotage you.

4. Look at the implications of being an in-time or through-time person. How could being aware of how you experience time influence your choices on a daily basis?

Key Idea

When obstacles appear this week, ask yourself, 'What do my values indicate that I should do?

3

Time is in the Balance

*The secret of life is balance and the absence of
balance is life's destruction*

HAZRAT INAYAT KHAN

Now that you understand how vitally important it
is to live in alignment with your personal values
in order to make the best use of your time, the next
thing is to begin to balance your values with what
needs to be done on a daily basis.

Here is a question for you. Do you have a balanced
life? Do you choose your pace, work with your natural
time clock and feel as if you are in rhythm with time?
If you do or you are getting there, congratulations –
you'll know what it's like to experience a balanced life.
However, increasing numbers of my clients tell me that
balance is exactly what's missing from their lives. They

long to find the time to do all that needs to be done and still have the time and space just to be themselves. They yearn to find that elusive place of calm where life flows with ease and without struggle. They want their careers and their private lives to balance effortlessly – well, who wouldn't? The fact that you are reading this book tells me that you would like this too. You have put a great deal of time and effort into getting where you are now and you deserve to take stock, re-evaluate and regain your balance so that you can make more time to live.

This chapter is designed to help you notice how life looks and feels when you are in or out of balance. That way you can plan to do what is necessary before you spiral out of control. I'm going to show you *how imbalance occurs, the reasons behind it and what you can do to regain your equilibrium*. If you know that your life is out of balance in a particular area right now, well spotted. It's far easier to redress the balance when you are conscious of what's not working.

Is it possible for you to live a truly balanced life? The first point to be aware of is that balance, like time, is in constant motion. We are always moving towards or away from balance. Just as you think you've levelled up the scales, something shifts and you are off kilter once again. The trick is to be familiar with what balance looks and feels like for you as an individual. Once you are clear about that then you have a yardstick to work with.

Let's play a game. I want you to stop right now and take this physical test so that you can experience imbalance and its results. Make sure you are in a safe space. Stand up and stretch your arms out wide. In the same position stand on tiptoe. Okay, now really stand on tiptoe. Now stand on tiptoe on one leg.

What happened? Did you lose your balance? Did you try to over-compensate by grabbing hold of something? What did you do to stay balanced?

When we are out of balance in certain areas of our lives we feel out of control. Some people regain balance by grabbing on to someone else to tell their troubles to, or turning to food, alcohol, cigarettes, drugs, sleep or TV. Many of us look to quick fixes. We need to regain balance at any cost, so that we can win back control of our lives. If we perceive we are losing control we end up with this reaction called stress.

STRESSED TIME

Stress is the word of the century (and a bit of the last). Although we all react differently to life situations, stress happens when we are out of balance and not living in alignment with our own personal values. Simply put, stress comes from doing too much of what makes you most uncomfortable. And, when you do this repeatedly you will react mentally and physically. The cycle works like this. You find you are drained of energy, your resistance is lowered and your immune system is under pressure. Your judgement and performance are impaired, you are less happy, less self-confident and ultimately you break down both mentally and physically. Everyone knows at least one person who has suffered in this way: one thing's for sure – I don't want it to be you.

There are so many causes of stress: life changes, such as moving house or job, marriage or divorce; family upsets and bereavements; too much responsibility or not enough; feeling undervalued in any area of your life, frustration in your career, or despondence about lack of work; deadlines; and anything else that goes against your personal values. I'm pretty sure you could add more to that list. The point is that they add up to a life that is out of balance. To eliminate stress from your life you need to be able to see clearly which areas are vulnerable to attack, so that you can take responsible action quickly.

Michael is a prime example of someone who lived exactly this kind of unbalanced lifestyle. Michael was living at 100 miles per hour. As a commodity broker in the City, where the price of goods changes literally every minute, he was always working to a deadline. Because he was trading globally, he would often arrive in his office at 6.30 a.m. or leave after midnight. His mobile phone was constantly turned on and his laptop felt like an extension of his right arm. The pace of his life eventually took its toll and resulted in mishaps and accidents. His twisted ankle was a result of leaping out of his chair to grab a fax from the machine behind him. His broken finger was a result of catching it in a door on his way to an urgent meeting. His stomach pains were due to eating the wrong foods on the go. Even though he was single and carefree, he had virtually no social life, no time to exercise or take walks on the beach near his home.

By the time Michael came to coaching he was 'stressed out' and more than ready to redress the balance. During the sessions that followed, Michael took the steps outlined below and changed his life. He now works at least one day a week from home and shares the very early and very late trading hours with his new business partner. Instead of working harder he is now working smarter and his partnership has resulted in increased revenue for the two of them and their company. Michael makes sure he combines exercise with fresh air and jogs daily on the beach. He is back in control of his life because he is now living a life that he has designed to give him more of what he wants. Michael regained his balance and learned how to be the master of his own time.

Take a moment now to identify your own stress-producing situations:

- What issue is causing your stress?
- Is there something else 'underneath' that?

- Is there anything else underneath that?
- What are your options for resolving your stress?
- Which options does your family/company/boss/ partner want you to try first?
- Which options do you want to try first?
- What strengths/resources are available to you to improve the situation?
- Which option will you choose to act upon?
- When will you do that?

BALANCED TIME

What did you discover from answering the questions above? Were you surprised at any of your answers? Any stressful situation has the ability to move you away from balance in your life. As we said, you are either moving towards balance or away from it, so I'd like us to get personal now and see exactly what balance looks like for you.

You may already be familiar with the Balance Wheel (or Wheel of Life as it's sometimes called). It's a fabulous tool that allows you to look at your life as a whole and then score how satisfied you are in each area. Satisfaction levels are different for everyone. What satisfies me will not necessarily satisfy you. There are no comparisons and no rights or wrongs. Rating your own personal satisfaction in each area of your life will allow you to look at your low-scoring areas and ask yourself what needs to be done to redress the balance and raise the scores. For instance in the career section your satisfaction might depend on how many hours you work, how valued you feel, whether you are doing a job that has meaning for you. Taking all this into account may give a satisfaction level score of six. Take a moment now to score your own satisfaction level in each area of your life, using our example as a guide, with zero being extremely dissatisfied and ten being completely satisfied. When you have scored each area join up the dots to create an inner wheel.

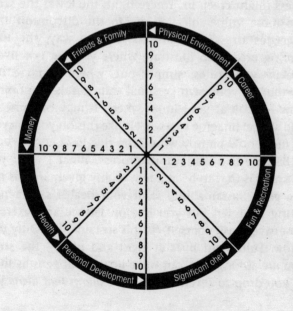

Physical environment: 1 2 3 4 5 6 7 8 9 10
Career: 1 2 3 4 5 6 7 8 9 10
Fun and recreation: 1 2 3 4 5 6 7 8 9 10
Significant other: 1 2 3 4 5 6 7 8 9 10
Personal development: 1 2 3 4 5 6 7 8 9 10
Health: 1 2 3 4 5 6 7 8 9 10
Money: 1 2 3 4 5 6 7 8 9 10
Friends and family: 1 2 3 4 5 6 7 8 9 10

What did you notice? Well done if you spotted that the low-scoring areas are also an indication of where stress might creep in. You're right: the lower the score the more vulnerable you are to the discomfort that precedes stressful situations. By the way, the low-scoring areas also illustrate where you are not living life by your rules; simply put, where you are not honouring your own personal values. Take a moment now to look at your inner wheel. It may be quite an odd shape. Imagine two wheels like this on your bicycle of life – how bumpy would the ride be?

Balance is a continuous process. What I want you to know is that to be at a ten, in any given area, is not the goal. Sustainability is. If your health satisfaction rating is at ten but you live on lettuce and exercise obsessively, ask yourself, 'Is this sustainable?' Only you know. Fulfilment lives at eight and nine – the score you are aiming for. Your wake-up call happens as soon as you drop to seven. *Seven is the alarm that alerts you to impending imbalance.* The beauty of the Balance Wheel is that if you check it regularly, you'll be aware of the movement and can address it quickly.

Guess what the worst rating is? No, it's not zero, it's five! If you have this score in any area, ask yourself, 'What's it like to live at a five?' Take a moment to listen to your answer. I'm pretty sure you've said something like, 'Boring, frustrating, resigned, neither really good or truly bad.' The thing is that five is neither painful enough to act upon nor pleasurable enough to want to keep the status quo. Five is simply mediocre. If I told you about a very mediocre restaurant I had been to and then invited you there for your birthday, would you want to go? If it were only possible for you to work in a mediocre job all your life, would you feel satisfied and fulfilled? Or if you could only go out to mediocre places or go on mediocre holidays and have mediocre relationships, would you be excited? Of course not.

You have far higher standards than mediocre. Check out your Balance Wheel and commit here and now to doing what it takes to raise those scores and move towards a life that measures up!

Once you recognise where your life is out of balance, you'll want it to change. So consciously commit to the discipline of rebalancing or accept the consequences. You see, you do choose whether to be in or out of balance with every response you make to what happens each day. When I began my new life as a single mother I was the first to say that it looked as if balance were not a choice. I just had to juggle work with family and all that entails. However at that level the quality of my life was much less than a five. There was far more time spent working than being a mum or anything else, come to that. I decided I was not willing to accept the status quo. The decisions I made to change my life did not meet with everyone's approval. Well-meaning family and friends expressed concern about my intentions and the changes I was making. I was not following the usual rules of practice and when one person changes the rules it can sometimes be uncomfortable for those around you. It can question how they are living their own lives and can even throw your relationships off balance for a while. Choosing change is radical. However, once they could see that I was serious and acting 'responsibly' around providing for my family and myself they climbed on board and gave me their respect and admiration. I am committed to having as much balance as it is humanly possible to achieve and that's exactly what I want for you.

BARRIE'S STORY

Barrie is the executive chairman of his own software services company and a person who likes to be in control of his own life. During our first coaching session, Barrie made an interesting discovery. Being in control means he does everything. Not only does he use his creative strengths to grow his company, he also manages admin, everyday management and is constantly available for all his staff. And no prizes for guessing who makes the decisions at home about the finances and the holidays. When Barrie came to coaching he was under pressure and overwhelmed. His time was taken up with so much day-to-day 'housework' that although his business was successful, he was becoming more and more stressed. Just six sessions into our programme, he regained clarity and focus and now feels more in control of his life than ever before. Having just come back from a three-week family trip to California, something almost unthinkable in the past, Barrie is delegating anything that pulls him away from what's most important to the company and is empowering his team to become more independent and use their considerable personal resources to push the company forward. His company is growing exponentially and yet Barrie is more focused, has less stress and is happier than he has been for many years.

One strategy we used so that Barrie could gain some perspective on how he was spending his time was to complete the following simple exercise, which I'd love to share with you.

TIME BALANCE EXERCISE

You'll need a clean sheet of A4 and a pen. On the left side of the page write the word Yes, on the right side of the page write the word No. Because we only have a limited amount of time in our time banks each day, it's vital to understand that every time we say 'Yes' to something, we are saying 'No' to something else. For example, if you say 'Yes' to working late, then you'll say 'No' to more time for you. If you say 'Yes' to working part-time you'll be saying 'No' to the nine-to-five routine. If you say 'Yes' to buying that new car you'll be saying 'No' to saving or investing.

It works vice versa too. Take another sheet and write the word No on the left-hand side and Yes on the right-hand side of the page. Run the exercise again from this perspective. Some people find it easier to go from No to Yes so try it both ways and notice the differences.

Now it should be clear just how much all your decisions cost you in terms of your time. If you work in a long hours culture, I want you to be very aware of what it's costing you in time to live this way. If you are willing to pay the price then great; if not it's time to redress the balance. Choosing to live in balance is a life-changing decision. It may impact other people, it may impact your finances, and it will impact your present and your future. In order to make this decision you have to know your outcome, how you want your life to look and what it would feel like to experience a balanced life every day.

This is exactly how I want you to envision your balanced life. Ask yourself these powerful questions and start painting a picture of your balanced life.

Balance Questions

- What would a balanced life look and feel like?
- What needs to happen in each area of my life to regain balance?
- What would I need to know about myself in order to regain my balance?
  (For example, am I a morning or evening person? Do I work well to planned deadlines? How many regular breaks do I need? What kind of support would I like?)

THE WORK

1. If your life were balanced right now what would you have to say 'No' to?

2. What one action could you take now that would increase the score in each area of your Balance Wheel? You know what it is – you've been aware of it for ages. Now's the time for action! Addressing the balance in just one area will impact all the others anyway, but my challenge to you is to take one action in each area and become the balanced and productive person you deserve to be.

Key Idea

Is what I am doing right now moving me towards or away from balance?

4

Productivity Under Pressure

*If I had eight hours to cut down a tree, I'd spend
six hours sharpening my axe*

ABRAHAM LINCOLN

Sounds like a lot of preparation for two hours' work. But Abraham Lincoln's plan was to get the job done in the shortest possible time. He knew how important it was to have that axe good and ready for the job at hand. He also knew that *focused planning* would treble his productivity. 'Failing to plan is planning to fail.' To make the time to live by your values and create balance in your life it is vital that you discover how the power of planning will be fundamental to your successful life management. Even when we know our outcome, have the right attitude and we are ready to take action, there will always be areas of our lives that we cannot control.

However, we can *always* control our own personal effectiveness in our daily lives by putting a few simple structures into place.

PERSONAL EFFECTIVENESS

I often wonder why it is that with so much available technology and labour-saving equipment, we nonetheless seem to have much less time to get things done. It doesn't matter whether we work in or out of our homes, there is always more to do than there is time to do it and the pressure is on many of us to do more with fewer resources. Everything is urgent and yet the goalposts keep moving. Many of us are just plain exhausted. We know we need to respond positively to what needs to be done and at the same time be aware of the energy-drainers, which make us ineffective. So how do we learn to dance on a shifting carpet, rather than have the rug pulled out from under us?

First you need to understand that personal effectiveness is a winning combination of 'being' and 'doing'. Here's the formula. *When who you are and what you do combine together, you will experience limitlessly high levels of productivity.* It's a very simple equation and in over twenty years of training personal development, I've never known the formula to fail.

Let's look at this in more depth by hearing Alex's story.

Alex is a highly creative designer in an advertising company. He recently won an award for his evocative visual image for a new men's fragrance. He always hits his deadlines for producing the artwork and is known for his reliability in this area. However, part of his work involves budgeting and liaising with the copywriters who put the words to the pictures. He is notoriously difficult to arrange meetings with and procrastinates endlessly about producing figures. As a result he experiences personal frustration and stress in these areas and is particularly unpopular with the finance department.

Alex is perfectly effective when he is working to his strengths; however he discovered that he becomes increasingly ineffective when asked to manage in areas that have less importance and meaning for him.

The truth is that real personal effectiveness, in or out of work, depends on the right formula of being and doing. As human beings we are constantly striving to attach meaning and purpose to our actions. Our ultimate goal is to be valued and be of value. As a result of becoming personally effective many people find this meaning and purpose in their lives and ultimately do work they love, enjoying balanced lives that fulfil them in every area.

On the way to this place, though, is the reality of where they are now and that isn't usually their ideal world. In many businesses it's not always financially possible to concentrate solely on your strengths. Like

Alex, many of us are being challenged daily to multi-task in different roles. In situations like this entrepreneurs and employees alike need to be able to manage more than just their main areas of expertise.

Julie's life situation is a classic example of the need to multi-task. Julie is a single parent juggling her work as a yoga teacher and her art studio with running her home and spending quality time with her children. Allocating time for everything and everybody is not a personal strength and so she finds herself running from one place to another, changing 'hats' along the way. In our busy lives this is not an unusual situation to find yourself in.

If you are being stretched in this way, it's especially important that you find a structure that will allow you to get everything done with as much ease as possible. Without a structure you will begin to experience stress and a feeling of being overwhelmed and then you'll get nothing done anyway. The only way to do this is to take the time to plan.

PLANNING AND PRIORITISING

If you've kept your time log consistently, you know where your time is going. You understand that with limited time each day you must focus your attention on what's most important or you'll have no time left for the rest of your life.

Armed with this knowledge, your next step is to create a structure that works each and every time you use it. Before we begin, though, it is vital that you understand the concept of planning.

Planning

This is going to sound incredibly simplistic but if you did nothing more than plan each day, every day, you'd already be well on the way to becoming powerfully effective with your time. Planning is about decisive not impulsive action. It's premeditated. It is also a choice. It's the art of bringing the future into the present so that something can be done about it now.

Charles Hobbs, the author of the 1970s book *Time Power*, said: 'Success is the consistent achievement of planned objectives, which are of value to the individual.'

Without a plan you will never realise your capabilities. You may have great vision, but it is your plan that will ultimately turn that vision into reality. The better your plan the more successful you will be.

Without a plan the chair you are sitting on could not have been put together, the building you are in could not have been built. Without a plan our country would not function (well, perhaps that's a little more controversial), certainly emergency services would experience daily disruption, companies would not run, holidays would not get booked, appointments would not be made and we would be living in a country called Chaos. Anyone you know living there?

In 1940s America, an efficiency expert named Ivy Lee paid a visit to Charles Schwab, who was the president of a new company called Bethlehem Steel. Their encounter has made it into numerous time-management books as a perfect example of the importance of simple planning. The story goes that Ivy Lee called upon Charles Schwab and told him that he could increase the company's efficiency and sales if he could spend just fifteen minutes with each of Schwab's executives. Obviously Schwab wanted to know how much that would cost him. Lee told him, 'Nothing, unless it works, and then you can send me a cheque for whatever you think it's worth, fair enough?'

Schwab agreed and Lee spent fifteen minutes with each of the executives in the struggling steel company and asked them to complete a single task. Lee requested that every evening for the next three months each executive was to make a list of the six most important things he had to do next day. Then the executive was to prioritise the tasks in order of importance. Lee told them to begin each day with the first item on the list and tick it off when completed. They were to work their way down the six items and if they didn't get something finished it was to go on to the next day's list.

By the end of the three-month period, sales and efficiency had increased to such an extent that Schwab sent Lee a cheque for $35,000, which in today's money would probably be $350,000!

The power of planning cannot be dismissed.

Spontaneous Time

Planning is not just about getting more things done. In fact you may choose to fill your time with a lot less than you do at present. You will always need some catch-up time, a morning or afternoon, when you just take a deep breath and regroup, file away old stuff and take stock of where you are. You need to plan some time to do this. If you fill up every hour of every day with things that need to be done you'll be trapped in your own structure and that's not what life management is all about. There has to be some time put aside for you to breathe, take a walk, and set your mind free to be spontaneous and creative. When you choose to focus all your concentration on what's most important you'll find that there is time for all of your life. However, the emphasis here is on 'choice'. Instead of reacting to situations, instead of working on a first-see, first-do basis; the choices you make about how you plan to spend your time will give you the clarity and focus to make your life work in balance.

Mind Your Language

Choice is a fabulous word. It implies that you have an option and that you are in control. There is a huge difference between what you have to do and what you choose to do. 'Have to' implies that someone else is in control; 'choice' means you get to choose. To compound this, 'choice' is what gets the job done every time. Here's something to consider. If your boss or a client, or even your partner asks you to do something that you don't really want to do but feel you 'have to' do, the likelihood is that you will put it off for as long as you can. If, however, you actually 'choose' to do the task, then the likelihood is that it will get done and on time. It's a simple matter of language, but changing your language will change your attitude to what needs to be done.

My request as your coach is that you set yourself a challenge this week. For every task that needs to be done, you affirm, 'I choose to do this,' rather than 'I have to do this.' Notice how different this is to your usual reaction and how you approach the task as a result.

Knowing how to plan will make an immediate difference to your time. The most successful people in the world have several things in common, among them that at some point they sit quietly, think and write down their plan for the day. They also have a specific formula for creating their plans: I will take you through this step by step so that you can put it into use now!

The first thing you'll need is an organiser or planner. It can be paper-based or electronic but it must have certain functions: it must show you a year at a glance, a month at a glance, and a day at a glance. A two-page per day organiser is best, so that you are not distracted by tomorrow or yesterday. It's so important to focus on the day ahead because you can only live one day at a time. If you are plagued by loose ends from Wednesday and today is Thursday where will your focus be? Even if you bring tasks forward from yesterday you are still focusing on today.

A planner is an exceptionally useful tool and you can use your imagination to make it work for you.

Lucy works for one of the top five corporations in London and has an exceedingly busy life. Lucy uses her planner to show clearly the balance of her life by entering work tasks and meetings in different coloured pens. Her social life shows up in yellow and as she works out of the office a great deal, these days are in red. So when Lucy looks at her month or year, at a glance she can see how her life is balancing up.

> The key to consistent success is Consistent Focused Daily Planning.

Planning time always involves writing things down. Not many people can keep more than three things in their head at the same time. Without my daily action list, I would be lost. Sometimes my mind is so full, I go upstairs to get something and completely forget what I went up for. I have to refocus and think hard, and even then I sometimes come down without the item I went to retrieve. I don't suffer from severe memory loss but if it is possible to forget in a few seconds the aim of a brief journey upstairs, it is entirely possible to forget appointments or meetings if they are not properly scheduled.

Life has a funny habit of throwing us off balance so easily. There is a fabulous saying: 'If you want to make God laugh, tell him your plans.' Clearly we cannot plan for every eventuality. Children fall ill when you have a vital meeting planned, planes get delayed and disrupt arrangements, papers do not always arrive on time for signature, and contracts rarely get exchanged when they are supposed to. We know this and yet we leave things to the last minute and then panic.

The joy of planning is that you prepare yourself in advance as much as possible and limit the damage that may arise. It's impossible to get it right every time, but nine times out of ten you'll have a much better chance of success if you plan.

Planning takes time. One company I worked with in Hull has taken on a planning culture. The whole company arrives at 7.15 a.m. and spends the next

fifteen minutes in quiet planning time. No one inter-
rupts anyone and everyone finds this time incredibly
empowering. They have all, of course, increased their
personal effectiveness. How fabulous to be supported
in this way. Perhaps you too could change the culture
in your company, but in the meantime you'll need to
choose to be disciplined and committed by yourself.

YOUR CONSISTENT FOCUSED DAILY PLANNING ROUTINE

You must take at least fifteen minutes each day to sit
quietly, to think and to write down your plan for the
day. If you want to achieve your goals and find time to
get things done then you must make the time for forward
planning. The right time will not magically present itself.
Your daily planning time is *vital* for your business and
personal success. Make sure you find a place where you
will not be disturbed and decide not to be distracted by
post, e-mails, telephone calls or other people.

There are only three things you need to know, which
when combined create the magic formula for success:

- What you want: the specific outcome you want to
  achieve
- Why you want it: what achieving this outcome
  would give you
- What plan of 'specific actions' will make it happen

> To make the right choices you must consistently direct
> your focus each day. It's not what you do once in a while
> that makes you effective, but what you do consistently
> that will shape your life

YOUR PRIORITISED DAILY ACTION LIST

I'm going to take you through an exercise that will
help you to create your daily action list.

Take a blank sheet of paper and imagine it's Monday.
We are going to create a wish list of everything you
need to get done this week. You'll need to write down
the projects that need attention, what targets need to
be reached, what personal goals you are working
towards and anything else you can think of.

You may want to divide your sheet between work
and home. We live a whole life and it's important to
discover just how much time we allocate to our work
and home life respectively. So, get as much down on
paper as possible.

Use these Powerful Focused Questions to assist you.
Ask yourself:

- Which task will give me the highest return on my
  investment of time?

- Which task, if I don't complete it, will be the greatest threat to my survival at work?
- Which task, if not completed, will have the greatest impact on my life outside work?
- Is there a deadline to work to?
- What wasn't completed yesterday that must be done today?
- What do my personal values suggest are most important?
- Will this task contribute to my long-range goals?

Prioritising the List

By now you probably have a very long list. Your next task is to decide how to prioritise the list. There are of course criteria for doing so, which could include the closeness of the deadline, the level of resources involved, the potential impact or benefit of doing the task, or the cost of not completing the task by the deadline.

In order to evaluate our priorities effectively we are going to use a simple strategy, which begins with our old friends Urgent and Important. If you have spent some time asking yourself the question, 'Is this urgent or important?' you are now beginning to understand the difference between the two. Would you be surprised if I told you that many people find it hard to make that distinction? Of course you are not one of them, but if this important difference has slipped your mind, go back to chapter 1 and revisit the distinction before reading on.

Great, so now you have that firmly imprinted, let's continue to prioritise further. We are going to use the simple Time to Live ABCD system to evaluate the importance of each task.

A=Urgent; B=Important; C=Some value;
and D=Dump it

However, just before you do that, there is something else you need to know. Only 20 per cent of your list can be A-rated. I can already hear you say, 'But they will all be As.' Of course they will and that's why we are going to adhere to the 80/20 principle.

It is a fact that only a small percentage of our input into anything produces the majority of results. This is called the Pareto Principle. Vilfredo Pareto was an Italian economist who studied the distribution of wealth in a variety of countries around 1900. He discovered a common phenomenon: a consistent minority – about 20 per cent of the people – controlled about 80 per cent of the wealth in Italy. Pareto called this a 'predictable imbalance'. It follows in sales that

80 per cent of your income comes from 20 per cent of your customers. In companies, 80 per cent of your problems arise from 20 per cent of your staff. When I pointed out to a distraught client who was planning her wedding that it looked like 80 per cent of her seating plan problems came from 20 per cent of her guests, she was surprised that this was almost exactly correct. While there may be argument for 60/40 or 90/10, the principle is broadly applied, especially in leadership and management, because it illustrates the notion that most of the results in life come from less but more focused input, either in terms of effort or people.

So the rule is that only 20 per cent of your list must be As based on the principle that 20 per cent of our productivity produces 80 per cent of the results! Go back to your list and judge it using the ABCD ratings against each task.

Now judge by urgency. Ask yourself: Do I have to do it today? This week? Or this month? And mark it accordingly.

Next, estimate the time each task will take. Be honest with yourself. Tasks often take much longer than we anticipate, so bigger projects must be broken down into bite-size pieces.

Peter had three months to complete his dissertation in applied engineering. He had to spend time researching material for the 7,000 words required. He also had a day job. The only way of getting it written was to break it down into manageable pieces. On average, 2,000 words took two weeks to compile and write. Peter broke the work down into outline, research and writing stages. He allocated half days at the weekends to the task. He finally finished the document two days before the deadline. When you are quite clear about how much time a task takes you have more control over it. I promise that you'll experience a lot less panic about meeting your deadline when you chunk tasks down in this way.

When you have estimated the time for each task, slot your As for tomorrow into your personal organiser and slot the remainder of your As, your Bs and Cs into your organiser on the appropriate dates. You are effectively making an appointment with yourself by allocating specific time slots throughout your week or month to complete your projects.

Tomorrow's list should now contain a mixture of As, Bs and Cs.

Repeat this formula every day!

THE WORK

1. **Take fifteen minutes** of focused planning time daily.

2. **Prioritise** using the Time to Live system.

3. Use the 20/80 principle.

4. Be sure to do at least one of your A tasks every day. Be disciplined about not letting a day go by without completing an A task.

Key Idea

At the end of each day, ask yourself, 'Which were my best spent hours today?'

5

The Time Thieves

*Time is really the only capital that any human being has,
and the only thing he can't afford to lose*

THOMAS EDISON

So, you've fine-tuned your attitude by understanding your values and motivation, you've started to focus on the tasks in your life and learned the vital distinction between urgent and important, as well as the crucial Time to Live ABCD method for effective prioritising. You're well on track to taming time! But no matter how well you've planned, every day insidious little monsters slide into your life with the sole intention of stealing your most precious asset, your time. They come in through the back door in the shape of people and tasks that get in your way. I call them the time thieves. Do you ever get the feeling that whole mornings or afternoons have been 'stolen' from you? Have you ended the day bemused, wondering where the hours disappeared to and berating yourself for your lack of productivity? No one is ever truly safe from the time thieves because they work subliminally. They arrive uninvited and before you know it you've been 'burgled' and there's no three-star policy to allow you to claim back the time. It's gone, never to return.

Only one tool has ever been effective in allowing you to take control of your time so that you can recognise and eliminate the time thieves. It's a way of noticing how your time gets taken from you and it's called 'The Art of Self-Management'. Self-management is key in mastering the time in your life. Unless you can trust yourself to create strong boundaries, and know when and what to say 'Yes' and 'No' to, those time thieves will get the better of you every day.

In order to discourage them, you need to stay focused on your outcome and become adept at communication. Whenever you open your mouth to speak, you have the power to move towards the life you want or move away from it. The power of language as a major asset in self-management cannot be underestimated. Unless you can articulate your needs honestly and responsibly you'll fall victim to the timewasters who would rather you did what they wanted instead of what you want. Self-management is a discipline that you must commit to. In my experience, however, many people wait until they are so put upon, so overwhelmed and so uncomfortable that they become self-managed as a means of survival. You are not one of those people. By recognising the pitfalls, you are able to anticipate and negotiate and manage your time. If you take a moment to think honestly, you probably already know what your own personal time thieves look like, but there may be some you have not yet identified. This chapter shines a light on them all and gives you simple strategies for eliminating them.

One thing's for sure: successful people are self-managed people who spend their time wisely. They know how much their time is worth both financially and emotionally and only invest it in what's most important.

PAID TIME

For those of you who exchange your time for money, the following analysis will let you know exactly how much your time is worth so you can decide where to invest it.

Time Cost Analysis

Take, for example, a person who earns £30,000 per year. Based on a fifty-two-week year, this equates to a weekly salary of £576.92. Based on a forty-hour week this gives an hourly rate of £14.42, which works out at 0.24 pence per minute.

Note, though, that these calculations are before tax deductions and daily expenses. When you add those into the equation, your value per year and pro rata down the line will decrease.

Take a pen and paper and a calculator and work through the following steps to discover exactly how much your time is worth.

1. What is your yearly salary?

2. Divide your yearly salary by fifty-two weeks to reveal your weekly salary.

3. Divide your weekly salary by forty hours to give you your hourly rate.

4. Finally, divide your hourly rate by sixty to give you your value per minute.

You may, of course, work more or less than a forty-hour week and you can change the calculations accordingly. Don't forget to add in your travel time too. As someone who is self-employed I realise that it's not just my paid hours that count as work time. It's not unusual for me to work a sixty-hour week even though my paid hours are less. I have my admin, my bookwork, the service I offer my clients in terms of e-mails and pre-session arrangements, preparation for trainings, and more besides. I need to spread my salary across all my working hours to get a true picture of how much my time is worth.

So now you have a true picture of your financial worth, are you surprised at the outcome? I imagine all kinds of thoughts have occurred to you as a result of this exercise.

PRICELESS TIME

What about those of us who do not measure our daily lives in financial terms? People like parents or carers who might have little or no income. If you are one of these people, your time is priceless time. It just cannot be equated to money. The emotional and physical energy you expend on a daily basis is immeasurable and my hope is that you derive satisfaction and personal fulfilment in all your daily tasks. You work with love and I have never found anyone who can put a price on that.

Whether you are paid or unpaid for what you do, however, you still need to focus on how much it costs you to waste your time on many 'low-yield' activities, which battle for your attention on a day-to-day basis. You see, however meticulously you plan your day, when the time thieves arrive you'd better be ready for them, and to do that you have to understand what they look like.

INTERRUPTED TIME

The time thieves present themselves in the form of interruptions. They test you out to see if they can sway your focus to possibly more appealing but less effective tasks. The average person gets one interruption every eight minutes or approximately seven per hour, or fifty to sixty per day. The average interruption takes five minutes, totalling about four hours or 50 per cent of the average work day. Eighty per cent of those interruptions are typically rated as 'little value' or 'no value', creating approximately three hours of wasted time per day.

There are only two types of interruptions: those that you can control, and those that you cannot.

Let me give you an example. Whenever I lead a time-management workshop, I introduce an exercise that makes the distinction between what we can and can't control. I ask the participants to pair up and give them a list of different scenarios to evaluate and answer. For instance, 'Can you control your health?' 'Can you control your staff?' 'Can you control the weather?' 'Can you control your family?' 'Can you control natural disasters?' And 'Can you control arriving at appointments on time?' There are roughly a dozen scenarios on the list and both people in each pair must agree on their final answer. This is the fun bit. Often the partners simply cannot agree. Some think you can control your staff and will tell you how, while their partners *know* that this is not true. Some partners make a convincing argument for controlling arriving at appointments on time and others make a good case for the opposite. After some discussion we come to this conclusion . . . the truth is that one of the things it's impossible to control is other people.

If you have ever moved house, you'll know how many people can be involved in the transaction from the initial seller to the last purchaser and how many situations can occur that hold up the whole process. Even if you've never moved house, I'll bet you have had to rely on another person or several other people at some time or another to complete a piece of work or get you some figures or have something signed and sent back to you. It can be so frustrating to have your own integrity threatened by someone else's failure to deliver. It's happened to us all and is a significant contributor to stress in the workplace.

You just cannot control other human beings and their actions. It's called free will and it began when Eve picked the apple off the tree. However, we do have the ability to choose our reaction to events at any given moment. Our resulting behaviour is influenced by our belief about what has happened, as we saw when we looked at beliefs. We have to accept that living and working with other human beings is unpredictable and often challenging. At work you can try to control them by communicating your needs effectively or by encouraging them in their role, but if they don't follow the rules you may try to control them by threatening them with dismissal, disciplining their behaviour, or imposing sanctions upon them. Socially, you can make ultimatums, be threatening or even withhold your affection, but ultimately tactics like these will fail. People always have the choice of staying or leaving. So it's clear that the only thing you can control is how you, personally, react to situations that occur every day of your life. And if the only thing you can control is your own reaction and resulting behaviour, the only thing that can ever stand in your way is yourself and your fear of the consequences.

Consequences are what stop us in our tracks. Fear can be a huge obstacle that blocks us from moving forward to do and be what we know we are capable of. Take a moment now to look at your own life. Ask yourself these questions:

- Where in my life do I compromise my values and myself because I am afraid of the consequences of my actions?

- What am I currently putting up with?
- What would have to happen in order for me to stop tolerating things the way they are?
- If there was no fear, what would I do?

I read a fabulous quote the other day, which said: 'Everything you want is on the other side of fear.' How many people do you know who waste a great deal of their time in fear?

Ready to get back in the driving seat of your life? Then let's look at what you can control:

You Can Control

- Inadequate planning
- Chatting on the phone
- Inability to say 'No'
- Procrastination
- Mistakes
- Unrealistic time estimates
- Mislaying important items
- Disorganisation
- Too much detail

Add at least five more of your own to this list.

What about interruptions that involve other people, the ones:

You Cannot Control

- Drop-in visitors
- Delayed decisions
- Weather
- Unnecessary post or e-mails
- Telephone calls
- Misunderstandings
- Undefined roles
- Overly long meetings
- Conflicting priorities
- IT problems

Add at least five more of your own to this list.

Of course there are techniques for handling the time thieves, which involve you taking deliberate action. These apply both to work and everyday life situations. Here are some tried and tested strategies that work.

Interruptions and Unsolicited Visitors

In the workplace, open-plan offices offer little privacy. If you have important work to focus on, how can you avoid interruption? You need to set some boundaries. Here's a suggestion: remember the 20/80 principle. Only 20 per cent of your tasks each day are vital. How about purchasing a wire photo-clip holder and writing

20 per cent in large numbers on a 3 x 5 card? Tell your colleagues that it means you're working on your vital 20%; don't abuse it and I can almost guarantee you'll get left alone and others will follow suit!

Quality Communication

Communication is vital for effective time management. Yet poor quality communication is one of the biggest challenges both in and out of work. The main point to make here is that people are not mind-readers. You may think you have expressed yourself clearly and yet people inevitably get the wrong end of the stick. You need to be absolutely clear when making requests or when you are given tasks, and in clarifying that you have understood what is required from you. There is nothing worse than producing a piece of your best work, only to find you had misunderstood the instructions, or running an errand for your partner only to come back with the wrong item. It's up to you to take personal responsibility for sending and receiving clear messages and there are no excuses on this one.

If anybody asks me what I do, I often say I'm in the question business. I spend hours every day just asking people questions. I never assume that I know the answers. My job is to ask laser-sharp questions, which will elicit the right answers from the only person who actually knows what they are: the client themselves.

Often I'll receive an answer that I don't und[erstand] I'll ask for further clarification. Take time to c[larify,] feed back what you think you have heard. I[f you are] wrong, then the other person will tell you, a[llowing] you to understand properly. It may take an ex[tra few] minutes to do this, but, boy, will you save yourself time and effort in the long run.

There is another fabulous tool for avoiding having other people's problems or work dumped on you; just say 'No'.

It sounds so easy, doesn't it, but 'No' can be an extremely challenging word to use. People attach their own personal meanings to it, such as that the person is 'unhelpful', 'not a team player', perhaps 'aggressive'. They think that promotion depends on them never saying 'No'. The truth is that the fear of saying 'No', however we justify it, actually means that we say 'Yes' too often.

You only have so much time in your time bank. Remember our Yes/No exercise. If you say 'Yes' to working late, you are saying 'No' to social life. Look back at your values. Is this how you want to spend your time, that precious time you can never get back again once it is spent? It is so vital to understand this, because not using this simple word is a major contributor to stress and illness. At the very least, it leaves you feeling overwhelmed.

There are, of course, ways of saying 'No' and it's important that you find the right language to do just at. 'I can't do it now, but I can do it later/tomorrow/ next year,' or, 'I'm working on the annual report and the budget, does this take priority?' are both ways of saying 'No' that don't mean you are avoiding the task.

Have you ever come across what I call the 'coffee machine syndrome'? This is what happens when people gather around the coffee machine, or in the kitchen to complain to other people about something. Nine times out of ten, no one present can do anything about the situation and everyone walks away feeling frustrated, angry and miserable. If you are familiar with this syndrome and are a good listener, I'll bet you've been dumped on many times. Isn't it draining and, quite honestly, simply boring?

In a situation where your good nature is being taken advantage of and you find yourself drawn into the soap opera of other people's lives, use of the word 'No' will definitely be required. Decide right now that you no longer have to waste life listening to 'dumpers'. Just decide to say 'No' to this stuff. Say 'No' in your mind and vote with your feet. Leave. The more you use the 'No' muscle, the more control you will have over your time.

What About the Telephone?

Remember we talked about 'urgent v important'? When the phone rings, it's urgent but not necessarily important. Unless it's your job to answer the phone or company policy insists you do, or even if you work alone, the phone can be managed and here's how.

When you must focus on an important task, use your voice-mail message as your personal assistant. Decide how much time you need to concentrate and leave a message letting callers know when you will check your calls. You may only need an hour. Most people can wait an hour; in case of an emergency in the workplace, tell a colleague to interrupt you or have your mobile close at hand.

When you need to make a call be prepared. Plan your calls and have any necessary information to hand; give a time limit for the call, if required. Because a great deal of my coaching is done over the phone, my clients always ring at their appointed time. My calls must run to time, otherwise I'll miss my next client. Often I will state at the beginning of my call, 'We have forty-five minutes; what would you like to focus on today?' By setting the boundaries of the call, clients know where they stand, and when we have around five minutes left, I tell them so that we can round things up instead of rushing to finish the call. Give this a try the next time you make a call and keep your watch by the phone. Take care though. You may not want to do this with a new boyfriend or girlfriend but you might want to with certain friends or family members who might otherwise talk for ever. Be imaginative in fighting the

ieves. Look for what you can say rather than
g on what you can't.

E-mails

E-mails are the number one reported distraction for
computer users. They are also one of the most time-
consuming activities you can indulge in. How many
times has an hour slipped by unnoticed while you read
and answer the contents of your mailbox? We've all
done it. I came home to 196 e-mails after a seven-day
holiday and I didn't think I even knew that many
people.

Here are some suggestions for handling the e-mail
time eater:

- Set specific times each day to check messages. Let
  senders know your routine. Early mornings and
  straight after lunch work quite well.
- Keep e-mails short. Use one main point per message.
  You are not writing a novel.
- Don't send joke messages or chainmail, ever.
- Keep e-mails professional at all times: e-mails with
  flirtatious connotations have a strange habit of circu-
  lating globally.
- Create subject files or delete e-mails regularly. There's
  nothing more distracting than a cluttered in-box.
- Always reply to e-mails within twenty-four hours. If

you don't they move down the in-box list and can
often get forgotten.

Meetings

> A committee is a group that keeps minutes
> and loses hours
>
> MILTON BERLE

Meetings that go on and on are so time-draining.
Studies show that the average manager spends about
seventeen hours a week in meetings, six hours planning them and untold hours in follow-up. I have a
client who spends most of his week in meetings; he
told me that as much as a third of the time is wasted
due to poor meeting management and lack of planning. Here's some of the best advice available to help
you achieve manageable meetings:

- Plan in advance and stick to the agenda. Make sure
  you understand the objectives and goals for the
  meeting and what contribution is expected from you.
- Start and finish on time.
- Do not meet in your own office; it's much easier to
  leave someone else's office than your own.
- Only attend if you have to – clarify in advance.
- Hold meetings standing up – they often end quickly!

- If the meeting runs over time and you are no longer needed, speak up. Ask to be excused.

Delegation

If you have ever walked into a chief executive's office you may have noticed that in 90 per cent of cases their desks are clean and empty. An old-fashioned expression comes to mind: 'You don't have a dog and bark yourself.' It's not that chief executives are lazy, they just know how to delegate. By employing the right people for the job, they are free to keep expanding their vision of their company. At some point they realised that being in control does not mean doing everything. Not only is that far too time-consuming it's also not an effective use of their time. The best managers in the world know that growing your team grows your business and creates higher morale and better staff retention. So now it's time for you to be chief executive of your own life. Take the following tips away with you and start to use them.

- A person must know why the job is being delegated, what must be achieved and when it must be finished. Once again, great communication skills are needed here. You must always reclarify so the person you are delegating to understands what needs to be done
- Delegating also gives you a chance to show how

much you trust those on your team. The more you trust your team the more they can grow. When someone believes that you can handle it, don't you feel yourself growing in stature and confidence? A surefire way of destroying enthusiasm is to watch over someone's shoulder during a challenging task. Live with differences. Not everyone will do the task the way you would do it. Be willing to give other ways a chance – you may learn some new techniques

- Part of delegating is coping with mistakes. We have all made mistakes, it's part of learning. One way of avoiding this in the early stages is to request review information along the way. If all else fails, make sure you acknowledge what went well and then reclarify your needs once again

- Delegation is a gift you give yourself and the other person. It's about using the best resources available so that the job gets done brilliantly, freeing up your time to do what you do best

Drop-in Visitors

Ever had someone say, 'Have you got a minute?' Is it ever a minute they want? Of course not. They've come to steal your time. Unless you've time on your hands, have some stock phrases available to discourage them. If you have five minutes then use your watch and stick to five minutes.

You may work in the kind of environment that encourages drop-in visits from clients. If this is the case then you must be prepared for interruptions to your work. When planning your day, make sure you account for the flexibility that you may need.

Self-imposed Distractions

Clutter

Did you know that every time you raise your head and notice other work cluttering your desk (shouting, 'Do me, do me!'), you experience a 5 per cent distraction rate? This can add up to forty-five minutes of wasted time each day costing you, and your company, money. Take a moment to look back at your 'minute rate' to see the exact cost. Amazing, isn't it? I challenge you from today onwards to keep on your desk only the things you use every day and the one task you are working on. I can almost hear you shouting, 'Impossible'. But I want you to try this out. When you work on only one task at a time, however little you do of that task before you have to stop, you will do the work much more effectively and you'll have the clarity to go on to the next task far more quickly.

This theory does not apply just to the workplace. In fact it's one of the simplest and most effective time-management tools there is. After my initial time-management class, it was the first thing I did and it had a profound impact on my concentration levels. I strongly suggest you try the 'one thing at a time' strategy and follow this up by always having a clean desk at the end of the day. Many offices have a 'clean desk policy' with staff getting 'fined' for leaving a messy workspace. Create your own 'clear head policy' and you'll really notice the difference it makes to your sanity!

Take my self-management quiz to discover how much clutter is currently in your life.

De-Cluttering Life Quick Quiz

Rate your satisfaction with your behaviour against the following statements on a scale of one to five. 1 = much less than I'd like, 2 = less than I'd like, 3 = a little bit less, 4 = about right, 5 = excellent.

Statement	Score
1. My office is clean and clutter-free.	
2. My wardrobes and drawers at home are tidy and clean and my clothes are fresh, ironed and hung away.	
3. My bills and paperwork are well organised and filed away neatly to allow easy retrieval.	
4. I am not irritated by anything in my home or work environment.	

5. I finish what I start and do not have loose ends such as projects, half-read books or business matters to attend to.

6. I have plenty of light, heat and fresh air around me.

7. My equipment and appliances all work well.

8. My plants and animals are flourishing.

9. My car is in good condition and is regularly serviced.

10. My work and home environments are cleaned weekly and there is nothing in those environments to harm me.

11. I don't waste my time with too much television.

12. I learn from my past experiences and am more aware of my actions on a daily basis.

13. I make time to pursue my passions.

14. I have let go of people and relationships that drain my energy or have a negative influence on me.

15. I do not gossip about others, judge or excessively criticise people.

16. I am aware of any limiting beliefs that are holding me back and I am taking action to resolve them.

17. I have forgiven those who have hurt me, inadvertently or not.

18. I regularly tell those close to me that I love them.

Maximum Score = 90

0–18 = lots of clutter to free yourself from
19–36 = quite a lot of clutter remaining
37–55 = pretty clear
56–72 = smooth operator
73–90 = wow!

Information

We live in a world of information overload so it's imperative that you are selective with your reading.

- Open your mail by the bin, keeping only the essential papers. Date them, file them or pass them on
- Business magazines or articles must be filed and a date and time scheduled for reading. Paper breeds paper. Be ruthless – your time is at stake!

Procrastination

> While we are postponing, life speeds by
>
> SENECA

That's exactly what happens when you procrastinate – nothing. Procrastination poisons time and kills it stone dead.

I have a client who says she is a fabulous procrastinator. She puts as much off as possible and justifies everything by using her 'as soon as' list. Her list looks something like this:

- As soon as I have enough time
- As soon as I have enough money
- As soon as the house is decorated
- As soon as I find the right job

And so it goes on. Here is what I know about getting things done: if you really want to do something, you'll find a way; if you don't, you'll find an excuse.

Procrastinators are not lazy people, they are people who are not telling themselves the truth about what they are doing. If you find yourself in a position of inertia ask yourself the following questions:

- Am I bored? If so what needs to be done?
- Is there a habit here that must be broken?
- Is this a job I value? If not, could it be passed to someone else?
- Am I overwhelmed? If so, who can help me with this?
- Do I doubt myself? If so, what would I need to believe to move forward?
- If I believed that, what would I be willing to do?
- When will I do it?

When all else fails, take Nike's advice; 'Just do it'!

Habits that hinder

Have you ever noticed yourself slowing down as you approach your goals? Have you ever almost stopped yourself before you start and then wondered why you don't achieve the goals you set? It's almost as if there is a missing link between your goals and their achievement. This missing link comes in the form of hindering habits that sabotage your success and steal your time, your energy and your motivation. These habits are close relatives of the time thieves, but they are even more insidious. They creep up on you in the form of something urgent that you've just remembered you must do, sudden tiredness, an urge to see that soap on TV, hunger pangs or anything else that automatically pops into your mind. This type of sabotage is the quiet killer of your best laid plans. Unless you are very conscious of these time gremlins, they will sneak up on you and grab your time from under your nose before you've even noticed.

I am certainly on 'nodding' terms with these little hinderers. While writing this book, I consumed approximately five cups of camomile tea per 1,000 words, had strong urges for fresh air and a brisk walk, and even felt tiredness hit me so hard I had to shut my eyes for twenty minutes – oh, all right forty-five. Of course, by then it was nearly time for whatever I was supposed to do next and before I knew it, another day had slipped by.

Here are some questions to help you handle hindering habits.

- Notice your pattern. What habits automatically kick in as soon as you begin an important task?
- What self-imposed interruptions do you invite in?
- In order to stop this self-sabotage, what would need to happen?
- What will you do to break these habits?

THE WORK

1. **Identify your time-management problems** using the material in this chapter as a starting point.

2. **Create your strategies** to control interruptions.

3. **Improve your personal organisation** by creating systems to deal with information and by using the 'clean desk' policy.

4. **Avoid procrastination**: decide and take action.

5. **Know when to ask for help** and do it with dignity and respect.

Key Idea

What's the best use of my time right now?

6

Getting to Goal

The past cannot be changed. The future is
still in your power!

BERNARD BERENSON

Now you've made it this far you'll have realised that
there is so much more to understanding time than
mere clock-watching. It's not just about how much
time you have, it's how you decide to spend it that
will either keep you on course or steer you off track.
The more consistently you focus your attention on
what's most important, the more likely you are to
achieve your goals. If you have already put the great
tools I have offered you into practice, you will be much
more organised on a daily basis. You'll know how to
plan, how to prioritise and you'll understand how your
values influence every choice you make. Now you are

ready to look to your future and create goals that inspire and motivate you.

The whole point of having goals is that they enable you to create time frames within which to achieve results. Having goals allows you to plot your own course in this game called life. If you don't do this you will end up playing someone else's game of life. I imagine you know plenty of people who know what they want. You may work for an organisation right now that has a strong sense of direction. Is it *your* direction, though? You may work for yourself and sometimes find yourself a bit lost or even just drifting. How well have you plotted your course? You may be in a relationship with someone who knows exactly what they want for the future; is it *your* future too?

Keep your own goals in mind all the time. Guess what happens if you don't have any goals? Nothing happens. Because there was nothing and nowhere to 'grow to'. There's a wonderful saying: 'Some people make things happen, some people watch things happen and some people say, "What happened"?' I don't want you to be one of the last. Goals give our lives meaning and allow us to acknowledge ourselves for going for gold. However wonderful it is to receive acknowledgement and respect from others, there is nothing more satisfying than the respect we have for ourselves when we achieve what we set out to do and we arrive there on time.

On New Year's Eve many people create goals they would like to achieve in the coming year. They try hard in January, but by February 80 per cent of those goals have disappeared into the ether. Their goals never stood a chance of coming to fruition because they had to *try* so hard to achieve them. Ever tried to diet? 'Tried' is the optimum word here. Anything you 'try' to do is guaranteed to be a struggle. In fact 'I tried' is the war cry of wimps. 'I tried to lose weight,' 'I tried to change my job,' 'I tried to make it work.' Either you did it or you didn't. There is no in-between. 'I tried' does not cut it in this life and it certainly is not good enough for you and me. The only difference between successful people and unsuccessful people is that unsuccessful people *try to do it*, while successful people *do it*. They take the actions necessary to make it happen. This is the only way to achieve anything in life and is especially true of your goals.

Spend a moment thinking of all the high-achievers you know. They could be entrepreneurs, they could be celebrities, they could be members of your own family or some of your friends. Whoever they are, they have achieved their outcomes because they set goals and then *immediately* took the necessary steps to make them happen. They didn't attain their goals overnight, because as any of them will tell you, overnight success is based on years of hard work. They were not just lucky either; there is no such thing as luck. They were prepared. And when preparedness meets opportunity, success is just around the corner. Successful achievement of your goals requires you to set your compass to four key elements:

- An inspiring vision based on your own personal values
- The motivation that makes it be a 'must have'
- Total and unswerving commitment
- The ability to take massive and immediate action

Every successful person understands that you must set inspiring goals that motivate you because these are the only kind that you are ever likely to achieve. Then you must follow through. You must commit to take immediate and massive action until you reach your goal.

SEEING IS BELIEVING: WHAT'S YOUR VISION?

> Logic will get you from A to B. Imagination will take you everywhere
>
> ALBERT EINSTEIN

Goals turn the invisible into the visible. To create a compelling future you first have to be able to see it in fabulous Technicolor. There are no guarantees that you'll get exactly what you pictured, but one thing's for sure: without some kind of vision I can guarantee that you'll get exactly what you have right now.

The secret of successful visioning is to be able to dream in pictures, rather like running a video of your future in your mind. Ask successful people how they got where they are now and they will all have taken different routes. All of them, however, will at some point in the conversation tell you that they 'always wanted' whatever their vision was. For some it was financial security, or to run a beautiful hotel by the sea, or to enhance the environment in some way, or to design the most beautiful houses. The picture looks different to each of them and along the way it may even change. To create this picture of the future you desire involves your creativity and imagination.

I want you to have more than a picture, though: I also want you to have a strategy to achieve it. One of the best examples of this combination is Professor Benjamin Zander, the brilliant founder of the Boston Philharmonic Orchestra. Professor Zander, who teaches the Creative Musicianship Degree Course for advanced music students, has a unique approach. Each year he welcomes his new students by declaring that he already knows that each of them will get an A. In fact he guarantees that they will get an A. He tells them that part of getting that A is to write him a letter. He says:

In the letter you are to imagine having just graduated with a first-class degree in Creative Musicianship. You will report what your goals *were*, how you achieved them, how many hours of practise you put in, what obstacles you came across and how you overcame them, what mistakes you made and how you corrected them, what advice you took and how you applied it, what impactful life lessons you learned along the way, what advice you now have to give other students and how are you going to use that first-class degree to advance your studies and career. Every student writes this letter and every student who commits to a plan of action and follows it through always achieves a well-earned A.

This is exactly how I want you to envision your future. Ask yourself the same powerful questions so you can start to visualise your goals. Here's a tried and tested exercise designed to allow you to see your future clearly so that you can take the actions necessary to bring your future into the present. You'll need pen and paper and a quiet comfortable place to sit for about half an hour.

Ready? Start dreaming. Dreaming is one thing that we are all good at. How many times have you spent the millions you 'might' win on the lottery? What did you do with it? Who did you share it with? Easy, isn't it.

So let's imagine that you have won the lottery of life. You can have anything you want, anything at all. Dream really big. There are no limitations, you cannot fail; you simply cannot lose in this game. Let's begin by asking this powerful question: 'If I could have everything I wanted what would it be?'

Be very specific. Give details, colours, sizes and locations; sounds and smells and tastes. Look at every area of your life; use your life Balance Wheel as a guide. Write down everything you've been dreaming of for years, everything you have ever wanted. Turn up the volume, bring it into focus in your mind and make it even clearer than before. Imagine yourself living this life, doing those things, being with those people. You may even have come up with something you never thought of before. Keep writing. Answer all the following questions: Where are you? What are you doing? Who is there with you? How is achieving this goal making an impact on your life? How is it impacting those around you? Want to experience it even more fully? Ask yourself: If this vision were a piece of music, what would it sound like? If it were a landscape what would it look like? If it were a smell, what would it smell like? And if it were a taste, what would it taste like? Keep writing until you have written down everything you have ever wanted; don't take your pen off the paper, dream big and see yourself living this fabulous life.

Wow, that is some list you have there. Take a

moment to see what you have created. Your vision is a picture of how your life will look when you have achieved your goals.

Now go back over your dream list and ask yourself:

- When I achieve these goals, which of my values will be satisfied and honoured?
- If I achieved my goals, would I still want what I'd got?
- Does my vision motivate and inspire me to create goals and take action?
- What massive action will I take to achieve my goals?
- When will I begin?

If the goal is not based on your personal values, even when you achieve it, it will hold little satisfaction for you. Although the journey towards achieving your vision is as important as the goal, one without the other is only half a job done. It's so important to know that any goal that is not built on a foundation of your own values is hard to achieve. It will always be a struggle, an uphill climb. Your goals need to reflect what you must have in your life, be it success, achievement, peace, security or adventure. If they don't, you can be sure they are what someone else wants for you: your partner, your family, the media or society.

The next stage is to discover how motivated you are to achieve these goals.

MOTIVATION

> Obstacles are those frightful things you see when you
> take your eyes off your goal
>
> HENRY FORD

There have been many times in your life when you
have been motivated to get the results you wanted and
been completely successful. Remember learning to
drive? My daughter, like many of us, is motivated to
learn as quickly as possible so that she can be fully
independent of me, buses and relying on other people
to take her places. Though she hates tests and exams,
her value of independence far outweighs her concerns
and obstacles that may stand in her way. Anything you
have ever truly wanted and then achieved happened
because you were motivated. Motivation is absolutely
key in determining whether you will work consistently
towards your goal. Without the right motivation, your
goal will be about as compelling as wading through
porridge.

Anything can be your motivator. You may place top
value on health. You know that if you achieve your
goal of losing weight, your back will no longer ache,
your knees will no longer carry the pressure of your
expanding waistband, and you'll feel more energetic

and alive. Is that a big enough motivator for you? Perhaps respect or status is important to you. If you reach your goal, others will hear of your success and will respect you for what you have achieved and you will receive the acknowledgement and status that will make you so proud. Maybe security or financial stability is important to you. If you are able to promote your business, or better your career, you'll receive the remuneration that will give you even greater opportunities for future security. Are you motivated to improve the relationships in your life and create new ones? Does your creativity compel you to live abroad where the colours and the sunshine inspire you? You may yearn to own your own yacht because the sense of freedom this would give you would be so pleasurable, or you may want to own a magazine so that you can have a voice about what happens in our world. Whatever your motivator is, it has to be utterly compelling. It cannot be vague or half-hearted. It must absorb and inspire you, hold your imagination and keep you on course even when the going gets tough.

Do you see how important your motivation is in achieving your goals? Will you be able to achieve your goals from 'I wish'? Absolutely not. You will only reach them from 'I will'. Motivation must be present at all times. If you lose sight of it for a moment, be aware that you have done so and get back on track immediately. You'll need to rerun the video of your vision. Get it back into focus and see it clearly. Only when you are absolutely certain that you simply must achieve your goal will your fabulous journey have begun. Every journey begins from complete committment to ultimate attainment, so here is what you'll need to know about personal commitment.

THE POWER OF COMMITMENT

Until one is committed,
there is hesitancy,
the chance to draw back
always ineffectiveness.

Concerning all acts of initiative (and creation)
there is one elementary truth,
the ignorance of which kills countless ideas
And splendid plans:

That the moment one definitely commits oneself,
then Providence moves too.
All sorts of things occur to help one
that would never otherwise have occurred.

A whole stream of events issues from the decision,
raising in one's favour
all manner of unforeseen incidents
and meetings and material assistance,

which no man could have dreamed
would have come his way.
I have learned a deep respect
For one of Goethe's couplets:

'Whatever you can do,
or dream you can,
begin it.
Boldness has genius,
Power and magic in it'

From *Scottish Himalayan Expedition*, W.H. Murray

The visions you have created for your future are massively motivating, but there will be no lasting success without your daily commitment to your vision.

One of the main reasons why some people fail to achieve their goals and get what they really want is that they never fully commit to concentrating their focus. Never underestimate what can be achieved with commitment: it will make your goal a must rather than a should. Whatever you decide to commit to will take you on a journey that will grow you immeasurably as a person. When you reach your goal, it won't end there. You'll have seen the impact the power of commitment has in your life and it will be a journey you will want to continue for the rest of your life.

FROM VISION TO ACTION

> Let us go forward together
>
> WINSTON CHURCHILL

You've created your own compelling vision, your motivation is powerful and your commitment is rock-solid; now you are ready to go from vision to action.

Goals connect your future visions to what needs to happen now, today and this week. It's only when you can make that connection that your goals come to fruition.

Remember, there are only three things you need to know about goal-setting:

- What you want: the specific outcome you want to achieve
- Why you want it: what achieving this outcome would give you
- What specific actions must be taken to make it happen?

Simple, isn't it. However, before you take your vision and turn it into an action plan, check out these useful guidelines which will help you to set effective goals.

- Express your goals positively. 'Create a cohesive team' is a much more inspiring goal than 'Stop being a weak manager'.
- Be precise: set precise goals by putting in dates, times and amounts so that you can measure your achievement. You will therefore know exactly when you have achieved your goal, so you can take complete satisfaction from having done so.
- Prioritising: when you have several goals, it's vital to give each a priority. This keeps you focused on what's most important and helps you to avoid feeling overwhelmed by too many goals.
- Always write down goals: this crystallises them and brings them into reality.
- Chunking down: keep the individual tasks, which are part of your overall goal, small and attainable. Your goal may be a large one and at first it may seem that you are not making progress towards it. Chunking down tasks into smaller, incremental goals will keep you motivated and give you more opportunities for celebration along the way.
- Personal Performance Goals: do not be dispirited by failing to reach your goal for reasons beyond your control. It may seem that people, circumstances and situations will all conspire to stop you at one time or another. Base your goal achievement on your own personal performance so that you can stay in control of your own goals and gain satisfaction from

reaching them. Attaining your goals is as much about who you are *being* as a person as it is about what you are *doing* to get there.

- Use your full skill set: it's great to know what to do but you must also do what you know. You are already a huge resource. You have skills and capabilities that have got you where you are today. Use them. Add them to your toolkit; every one of them will be useful to you.

- Set honest goals: by all means set your sights high, that's the whole point, but also anticipate obstacles. Don't set yourself up for failure. Be honest with yourself about which skills you may need to master to achieve a particular level of performance.

- Set challenging goals: just as it is important to be honest about your goals and not set them unrealistically high, do not set them too low. People often tend to do what they know and play too small. It may be that they are afraid of failure or even success, or perhaps they are just too lazy! Always set goals that are slightly out of your immediate comfort zone, that will help you stretch and grow. Set exciting, challenging goals and welcome the occasional 'crash' that inevitably accompanies this kind of courageous striving.

You are in total control of your goals for the future. You already have the qualities it takes to succeed. Self-responsibility has brought you this far and self-responsibility will lead you to achieve your goals. Whatever you do today will take you towards those goals for tomorrow.

You now know that there are only three places to look:

- Where you are now
- Where you want to be
- The gap in-between

The gap has three bus stops. The first stop is called 'immediate'. It's what you can do on a daily basis to travel towards the next stop called 'intermediate'. By intermediate you are at least halfway, if not more, towards your goal. When you reach the 'long range' bus stop you have arrived at your destination.

Go back to your dream list. We are going to prioritise your goals. Have you checked to see that they align with your values? Are you motivated and committed to achieving your outcome? Okay, now you are ready to decide when you expect to get results.

1. Pick three goals from your list that you *must* achieve this year, and write them out on a separate sheet.

2. Create a blank time line for yourself, such as January–March, April–June. Decide which goals will be

achieved within six months, which within a year. Notice how you have prioritised your list. Did you want to do everything all at once or did you spread your goals over the year?

3. A goal is a specific measurable result so it is written in a certain way. It always has an action, a specific measure and it is time-dated. For example:

- Increase income by 30 per cent by this time next year (whatever that date may be)
- Earn promotion to board level by this time next year
- Buy a house in Florida by July next year

The reasons we have called our immediate, intermediate and long range goals bus stops is because they are just that, landmarks to use as you move forward in life. There is always another place to go and another route to take after goal achievement. Goals are a way of measuring progress and evaluating the effectiveness of your actions.

Now that you have three main goals that are specific, measurable and dated, you'll need to plan your actions so that you can achieve them. Work out where you will need to be and what you will need to achieve by the intermediate stop. Create an action list so that you can begin to see what actions will need to be taken each day to bring you nearer to your goal.

Use your Consistent Daily Planning Routine as your guide to what actions from your action list must go on your daily list and what actions need to be diarised or delegated. Remember your 20/80 principles and make sure you commit to planning every day so that you consistently do what it takes to live your dreams.

These are the keys to goal-making. This formula must become your mantra each time you set a goal. Live consciously every minute of every day; remember, you choose your success, so what are you waiting for – get out there and do it.

TIME TO REVIEW

After having achieved your goal, it's a good idea to review the process and its impact on the rest of your goal plans.

- If you achieved the goal too easily, make your next goals harder
- If the goal took a demotivating length of time to achieve, make the next goals a little easier
- If you learned something that you can use to change other goals, do so. If while achieving the goal you noticed a deficit in your skills, decide whether to set goals to fix this

If you do not reach your goal by the time limit you've set yourself, it's an opportunity to consider:

- Were you truly committed to that goal? It's fine if you're not. It was your goal in the first place!
- Were the actions that you took appropriate? (There's no point driving south to Bournemouth if you are in London and trying to get to Scotland)

Thomas Edison said, 'Just because something doesn't do what you planned it to do doesn't mean it's useless.'

It's the same with your goals. It doesn't matter if you fail to reach your planned goal, just as long as you learn from it. Take the lessons learned and feed them back into your goals-setting process.

Remember that your goals will change as you mature, so you'll need to adjust them regularly to reflect your personal growth. Goal-setting is your servant, not your master, and goals should always bring you real pleasure, satisfaction and a sense of achievement.

When you've got to grips with time, learned consistent persistence, thrown off your hindering habits, locked out the time thieves and achieved the goal you chose within the timescale set, celebrate immediately! Don't wait for others to pat you on the back. You are quite capable of giving yourself a well-deserved treat; no one knows what you enjoy more than you do, so get out there and have some fabulous fun – you have earned it.

THE WORK

1. Always align your goals with your values.

2. Create a compelling vision that will inspire you to achieve your goal.

3. Get totally committed.

4. Create an attitude of consistent persistence and get into action!

Key idea

'Great goals are compelling, vaguely conceived goals are vaguely manifested. Which kind are my goals?

7

Creating Sustainable Success

The secret of success in life is for a person to be ready for opportunity when it comes.

BENJAMIN DISRAELI

I believe you make your own luck and for me, luck happens when preparedness meets opportunity. You are now prepared; you have lasted the course. You have a blueprint that will allow you to become a master of your time. By understanding your emotional response to what happens every moment of your day, you can balance your work and your life so that you spend your time in a way that is more productive and fulfilling. Your challenge now lies in creating sustainable strategies, which allow you to maintain momentum on a daily basis. I know you are serious about creating more time and I applaud you for having the commitment to do what it takes to live a balanced, fulfilled and less stressed life.

I also want you to know from the outset that maintaining your time-management muscle is like maintaining any other muscle. It needs consistent exercise if it is to function properly. So many people are excited at the beginning of a new challenge. They wake up on a Monday morning determined that this is their week for change. They say enough is enough; they are no longer willing to tolerate the status quo. They are fired up and raring to go. However, by Wednesday it's all becoming a bit like hard work and by Friday? Well, it's nearly the weekend so they justify their lapses by promising themselves they will begin again on Monday. What stops them? What gremlin steps in just as they are stepping out to play a bigger game? If you are serious about successfully managing your time, you'll want to eliminate this kind of behaviour, which will sabotage your plans before you've even got going.

If you have discovered a new way of approaching challenges before, tried it for a while and then given up, you'll know how frustrating it is to be almost there and then wreck your efforts by not sustaining them.

It's time to make sustainable choices that motivate you and lead to success in all you do. To become master of your time, you will need to make these sustainable choices in every area of your life. The life-changing principles and tools you have been given so far will allow you to become self-managed and in control of your own time. To support you further in breaking through any barriers that stand in your way, this chapter gives you a selection of strategies to keep you on track and successful on a daily basis.

Every one of the suggestions in this book will work if you simply commit to taking the actions necessary. But whatever you do must be sustainable over the long term. As we discussed, that means whatever your goals, they must be in alignment with your values. Your highest form of personal motivation is your values. If the going gets tough or there are some difficult choices to make, it will be your values that will give you the answers you need to enable you to sustain successful goal achievement. Let me give you an example.

ANNIE'S STORY

Annie came to coaching to focus on her vision for the future of South Africa. She has a clear idea of the type of training required that will create a huge attitude shift around what is now possible for black people in her country. She passionately wants to achieve her goal to be part of creating this, but her family and her life is here in the UK for at least the next three years. Annie values her relationship with her family above all else. She knows that to work between the UK and South Africa will certainly impact the time she spends with her husband and children. It's vital that she creates a sustainable goal that honours her values and yet allows her to contribute in a way that is meaningful for her and those she wishes to help. By figuring out what's most important to her and working from this base-line, she can decide how much time to give to this project. She does not want to get involved in something she cannot maintain and let anyone down.

I pointed out to Annie that she'll need to plan this carefully and be sure about what she is saying 'Yes' to and what she is saying 'No' to. She must anticipate the challenges ahead and make sure she does not overly compromise her values, especially her value of family. Annie was prepared to do all this and then take the actions necessary to make her life work, aware that success depended on a sustainable way of operating. However, after some deep soul searching and careful thinking about her plan, Annie realised what she really wanted right now. She sent me a beautiful card that expressed how our work had made her understand that 'all she needed to know for now was just under her nose'.

Annie had decided that even though her vision for her country is as strong as ever, right now she wants to spend her precious time with her family. Her contribution to them and the fulfilment she gains from being present as much as she can in their lives is of paramount importance to her. If she had pursued her vision and compromised her values, she would never have achieved her goal. The future may be a different story, but for now Annie lives in the present, her present.

TIME TO LIVE

This is not just about the time in your life; it's about the life in your time. It's about making choices about who you want to be every day of your life. After all, we are human beings not human doings.

Accomplishing your goals is a great way to spend your time, but be sure that as you climb the ladder of success, it is leaning against the right wall. Take as much time to evaluate what you'll have when you have achieved your goal as you do in creating the goal in the first place.

I want you to be able to make choices on a daily basis that support you, so I have designed the following Top Time Checks to keep you on track as you become more and more successful with your time. Think of them as an extended version of The Work from previous chapters and use them as a pick 'n' mix of tips and tactics to combine with all you have learned throughout this book. In that way you will create sustainable success and make more time to live.

TOP TIP 1: LIVE INTENTIONALLY

Begin each day by setting your intention for the day. What do I mean by that? Decide 'how' you want to live the day ahead. For example, 'My intention for today is to live it without struggle and with ease.' This means that whatever happens and whoever I meet throughout my day, my intention is to have it be easy. In order to remind myself of my intention I'll need to keep asking a Powerful Focused Question. With my intention in mind, my Powerful Focused Question for today is, 'How can I have this be easy?' Guess what happens each time I ask this question? That's right. I find another way of doing a task or being in communication that is much easier.

TOP TIP 2: DO IT WITH ATTITUDE

Build in some enthusiasm by listening to some motivational music or tapes first thing in the morning and then decide on your attitude for the day. Will you be inspired, peaceful, fun, motivational, determined, focused? What do you choose? Carry this attitude with you throughout your day, and notice how it affects your work, your colleagues, your family and friends. Take a deep breath and get into action!

TOP TIP 3: DO IT YOUR WAY

Make sure you live each day in alignment with your values. Every time you feel upset, out of control or stressed, look to see which of your values is not being honoured and choose to take the actions necessary to rehonour them. Nothing will take you 'out of time' quicker than being 'out of sync' with your values. Minutes turn into hours and whole days get wasted. Get back in alignment and live consciously in each moment!

TOP TIP 4: STAY FOCUSED

Keep to your daily action plan, which you learned how to do in chapter 4. I cannot reiterate enough the importance of consistent focused daily planning. Take that time each morning to assess your day and plan to get the results you want. Do your vitally important As every day. This is a complete cure for procrastination – it gets the most important jobs done, leaving you more time to live!

TOP TIP 5: CREATE CLARITY

Don't assume lack of communication is someone else's fault. Take control by listening, clarifying and feeding back what's been said. Don't waste time having to redo tasks because you did not fully understand what someone else meant. Be responsible around communication!

TOP TIP 6: SUCCESS STRATEGIES

The ultimate success formula is to repeat what works. When you last got the most out of the hours in your day, how did you do that? What formula did you follow? Examine exactly what you did to achieve that high level of productivity, whether it was on a particular project, task, to get a promotion or even pass your driving test. Ask yourself, 'Who was I being to get that result?' Inspect your method for achieving results and keep repeating what works and make more time to live.

TOP TIP 7: I'VE STARTED SO I'LL FINISH . . .

Finish what you start. Give yourself a deadline. You can greatly increase your personal effectiveness if you make deadlines for each task, diarise when you'll do them and stick to it. Remember Peter in chapter 4? In writing his dissertation he had to meet a deadline. It was vital that he diarised time to work on it, planning out his chapters and how much time they would take. Peter reported that he noticed immediately that he was only capable of concentrating for a certain amount of time. This meant he had to work out how long he would need for completion. Because he had to fit this in around his job, he had to plan his time carefully over several months so that he could balance every area of his life with his writing. This really worked in his favour. Instead of spending all day writing, he would spend the morning writing and researching, because he concentrates best then, and use the rest of his time for whatever else he wanted to do. He reached his deadline and still had time to live.

TOP TIP 8: TIME TO BALANCE

Each individual has a peak time of day when their energy is at its highest and concentration at its best. Determine which time of day is your peak performance time and plan your work accordingly. Keep meetings and routine tasks for the other parts of the day.

Take an inventory of your sleeping and eating patterns. Look at your life over a two-week period and notice what works for you. How many hours' sleep do you need to function efficiently each day? What kind of food makes you feel fantastic and what kind leaves you with less energy, feeling sluggish or lethargic?

TOP TIP 9: DON'T WAIT, ANTICIPATE!

The power of anticipation cannot be underestimated. Before going full steam ahead with anything new, spend some thinking time anticipating the challenges that could arise. This applies to any new project, your health, a change of career or new relationships. While you cannot cover all bases, you may be able to avoid a crisis by giving yourself advance warning of what might lie ahead. The more practised you become at this the further ahead you are able to look.

TOP TIP 10: BECOME AN SRN AND STOP RIGHT NOW

SRNs are never late for anything. They get to meetings on time and they are ready on time. Ninety-nine per cent of the time they show up when they say they will. How do they do it? They know when to 'stop right now'. This works on a time-line system. You need to meet a potential client in town at 6.30 p.m. Traffic is busy at this time so you'll actually need an hour to do the forty-minute journey. So you stop work at 5.30, leave the office at 5.45 and get to your appointment late, stressed and apologetic. You know you left an hour for a forty-minute journey so what happened? Clearly, it takes you a good ten minutes to shut down your computer, clear up your desk and leave the office and that's without any last-minute interruptions. Therefore your stop right now time should actually have been 5.15 p.m. at the latest. Become an SRN and learn when to stop right now.

TOP TIP 11: VAT – VALUE ADDED TIME

Use this strategy to extract value added time whenever you can. Get into the habit of carrying a book, a Walkman or Ipod or your personal organiser with you. Use any spare moments when waiting for appointments, or travelling on the train, adding value to your time by enjoying some relaxing music, reading an absorbing book or working on your life list and planning ahead. Here's a fascinating fact. By taking one hour per day for independent study, seven hours per week, 365 hours in one year, you could learn at the rate of a full-time student. In three to five years, the average person can become an expert in the topic of their choice by spending only *one hour* per day. Always be prepared and plan to use any spare time by making it value added time.

Another way of adding value to your time is to think in terms of 'buying' time. The more hectic your schedule, the more reasonable it is to buy yourself time by selecting goods and services that save you from 'spending' your own time. Paying someone to mow your lawn or clean your house are examples of buying time. Think of some other ways that could buy you more time to live.

TOP TIP 12: BECOME SELF-MANAGED

You have an inexhaustible supply of potential within you. All you need to do is keep using your natural abilities and talents and watch yourself grow as you develop them every day. When you do this you will realise that you are becoming more and more self-managed. You'll recognise how much control you have over your time during the day and how much impact this will have on your destiny. As you begin to grow in self-confidence, your self-sabotaging tactics will decrease. You'll focus on your strengths not your weaknesses. You'll stop criticising yourself and instead start congratulating yourself on what you've achieved and how far you have come. You are a unique person. You have a unique set of values to live by.

From this moment on, I want you to see yourself as you really want to be. Step by step, break your old habits that have held you back in the past. The best thing about being really focused in the now is that you get to choose who you want to be again and again. Be sure to make choices that serve who you are now. Make choices that align with your values and allow you to be your very best. Imagine if you increased your effectiveness each day by a mere 1 per cent. If you did this consistently over a year, you will have improved by 365 per cent. How different would your life look then?

What would other people notice about you? How much would you be achieving?

Having more time to live means living consciously every minute of every day. That doesn't just happen by chance. Being prepared in any part of your life is what's needed, so that when your own opportunity comes along you are ready to show the world who you are. People who are prepared plan for the future and are prepared for success. Doing what it takes to make time to be who you really are gives you more time to live this wonderful life.

We are here to develop our potential and use all our natural resources to become self-reliant and self-managed. You are not your past or your conditioning. You are today exactly who you have chosen to be and you can choose again in every moment. The more self-reliant you become and the more responsibility you take for yourself, the more self-managed your life will be. There will be no blame, no justifications, less procrastination and much more action. You will know that it's down to you this lifetime around. In the midst of a chaotic world, you can discover safety and certainty in your own self, in a solid core of self-reliance. You only truly have control over how you choose to react to what happens moment by moment. Don't be distracted or put off by other people, situations or circumstances. Hold on to your vision and stay focused.

Stay true to yourself and your goals, honour your values, maintain your natural balance and know that you were born to succeed.

Key Idea

And my final thought for you is this, just make time to live and:

> Take heart,
> truth and happiness
> will get you in the end.
>
> You can't lose in this game.
>
> Have fun.
>
> It goes on too long
> to be taken seriously
> all the time.

From 'Eyes of the Beholder', John and Lyn St Clair Thomas

HODDER
MOBIUS

**Transform your life
with Hodder Mobius**

For the latest information on the best in
Spirituality, Self-Help,
Health & Wellbeing and Parenting,

visit our website
www.hoddermobius.com